ENGLISH in the Bag
(Inglés en La Bolsa)

A Fun & Friendly Guide to Learning English
for Spanish Speakers

By
Kecia Beasley Lindsey, MA

DISCLAIMER NOTICE:

This book was designed in accordance with the Common European Framework of Reference for Languages. Please note that the information contained in this book is for educational and entertainment purposes only. Every effort has been made to present accurate, up to date, reliable, and complete information. No warranties of any kind are declared or implied. Readers acknowledge that the author is not engaged in the rendering of legal, financial, medical, or professional advice. The content within this book has been derived from various sources.

By reading this book, the reader agrees that under no circumstances is the author responsible for any losses, either direct or indirect, that are incurred as a result of the use of the information contained within this book, including but not limited to errors, omissions, or inaccuracies.

AI-GENERATED CONTENT DISCLOSURE:

This book includes graphical content generated by AI and reviewed by humans

COVER CREDIT: Cindy Kibbe/Kibbe Creative Media, LLC

ISBN 979-8-218-93571-9

Published in the United States by EnglishandSpanish2You.com

www.EnglishandSpanish2You.com

DEDICATION

This book is dedicated to my parents, Oscar and Virginia Beasley, and to my Aunt Eloise and Aunt Barbara, who encouraged me to follow my dreams about expressing my love for learning languages.

INTRODUCTION

ENGLISH in the Bag is designed to provide children and adults with the ability to learn English conversation and the capacity to master spoken English. Learners of all ages can acquire oral English skills through practicing authentic scenarios based on real experiences native speakers would have. At every step, this book allows students to assess their English proficiency through the question-and-answer method and discrete written language activities. This book gives students the foundation they will need to move from beginning to intermediate, and finally, to advanced-level English.

ENGLISH in the Bag is founded on the key principles of Stephen Krashen's Comprehensible Input Hypothesis (i+1) and supports his philosophy that having "compelling content" is essential to learning languages:

> *"Learners acquire language by receiving input (listening/reading) that contains Structures slightly beyond their current level (i), which they can understand due to context and prior knowledge (the '+1')". ... "Input should be interesting and engaging enough to hold the learner's attention, making them forget they are in another language."*
> (Principles and Practice in Second Language Acquisition, 1982).

Language acquisition is a subconscious process, not unlike the way a child learns language. Language acquirers are not consciously aware of the grammatical rules of the language but rather develop a feel for correctness. Krashen writes, "In non-technical language, acquisition is 'picking up' a language."

TABLE OF CONTENTS

CHAPTER 4 Beginning English Grammar: The Simple Tenses

CHAPTER 5 Intermediate English Grammar: The Progressive Tenses 77

CHAPTER 8 Advanced English Grammar: Conditional Verb Tenses 114

CHAPTER 1
Greetings in English

LESSON 1.1: Greetings in English

Below is a table showing greetings in English—both formal and informal—along with their Spanish translations:

English Greeting	Formality	Spanish Translation
Hello	Formal/Neutral	Hola
Hi	Informal	Hola
Good morning	Formal	Buenos días
Good afternoon	Formal	Buenas tardes
Good evening	Formal	Buenas noches
Good night	Informal	Buenas noches
What's up?	Very Informal	¿Qué tal? / ¿Qué pasa?
How do you do?	Very Formal	¿Cómo está usted?
How are you?	Neutral	¿Cómo estás?
How's it going?	Informal	¿Cómo va? / ¿Qué tal?
Pleased to meet you.	Formal	Encantado/a de conocerle
Nice to meet you.	Neutral	Mucho gusto / Encantado/a

Activity 1.1: Practicing Informal Conversations

Directions: Read the informal English dialogue between two friends at the supermarket.

Rita: Hi, Jack! What a surprise!

Jack: Rita! It is so good to see you!

Rita: Same here. It's been such a long time. How are you?

Jack: I'm fine. Just picking up some snacks. And you?

Rita: I am good. I needed a few things for dinner.

Jack: Cool! Let's catch up soon.

Rita: Absolutely. See you later.

Jack: Good-bye.

Activity 1.2: Practicing Formal Conversations

Directions: Read the formal English dialogue of a professor greeting a student.

Professor Lewis: Good morning, Ms. Carter.

Student: Good morning, Professor Lewis.

Professor Lewis: How are you today?

Student: I'm well, thank you. And you?

Professor Lewis: I'm doing well, thank you. Are you ready for the presentation?

Student: Yes, I've been preparing all week.

Professor Lewis: Excellent. I look forward to it.

Student: Thank you!

Professor Lewis: You're welcome.

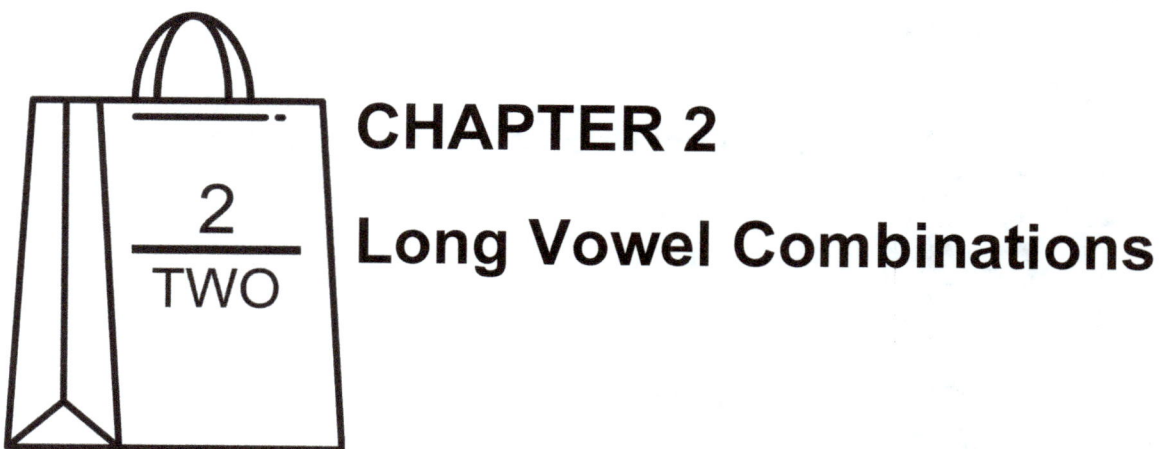

CHAPTER 2
Long Vowel Combinations

LESSON 2.1: Pronunciation of Long Vowel Sound

There are 28 long vowel combinations in the English language. They stem from these vowels: a, e, i, o, and u.

Let's pronounce the English long vowel combinations, focusing on their sounds and the formation of the mouth.

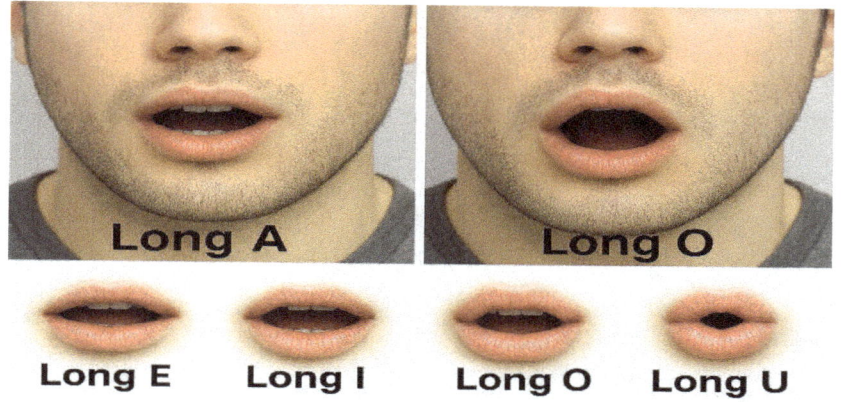

The table below has long vowels in English, including example words and simple picture ideas to help visualize each sound.

English Long Vowel Sounds

Long Vowel Sound	Spelling Pattern	Example Word	Picture Idea
Long "a"	a, ai, ay, a_e	cake	
Long "e"	e, ea, ee	tree	
Long "i"	ie, i_e, igh, y	kite	
Long "o"	oa, ow, o_e,	boat	
Long "u"	ue, u_e, ew	cube	

LESSON 2.2: Pronouncing the Long Vowel Combinations

English vowel combinations (also called vowel teams, digraphs, and trigraphs) are two or more vowels working together to create a single vowel sound.

English Vowel Combinations

Vowel Combination	Example Word(s)	Picture Idea(s)
al	palm	
au	applaud	
augh	laugh	
aw	saw	
ay	bluejay	

Vowel Combination	Example Word(s)	Picture Idea(s)
a_e	flame	
ee	bee	
ei	eight	
ew	jewel	
ey	key	
ie	pie	
igh	light	

Vowel Combination	Example Word(s)	Picture Idea(s)
oa	coat	
oe	toe	
oi	coin	
oo	moon, book	
ou	cloud, gouda, young	
ough	dough, cough	

Vowel Combination	Example Word(s)	Picture Idea(s)
ow	cow, bow	
oy	boy	
ue	blue	
ui	suit	

LESSON 2.3: Long "a" Vowel Combinations Grouped by Sound: ai, ay, a_e, eigh, ei

✏️ **Learner Tip:**

- **ai** appears in the **middle** (e.g., *rain*).

- **ay** appears at the **end** (e.g., *play*).

- Use the "magic e" rule for **a_e** (e.g., *cake*).

Example Words:

- **ai:** rain, train

- **ay:** play, stay

- **a_e:** bake, name

- **eigh:** eight, weight

- **ei:** vein, sleigh

LESSON 2.4: Long "e" Vowel Combinations Grouped by Sound: ea, ee, ei, ey, ie

✏️ **Learner Tip:**

- The most common Long "e" vowel combinations are "**ea**" and "**ee**".

Example Words:

- **ea:** eat, beat

- **ee:** tree, sleep

- **ei:** receive

- **ey:** key, monkey

- **ie:** chief

LESSON 2.5: Long "i" Vowel Combinations Grouped by Sound: ie, igh, i_e, y

✏️ **Learner Tip:**

- **igh** often in the middle (e.g., *light*).

- **y** at the end of words (e.g., *cry*).

Example Words:

- **ie:** pie, die

- **igh:** light, night

- **i_e:** time, ride

- **y:** fly, cry

LESSON 2.6: Long "o" Vowel Combinations Grouped by Sound: oa, oe, ow, o_e

✏️ **Learner Tip:**

- When "e" is at the end of a word using the "o_e" vowel combination, the "o" is a long "o" sound. This is known as the **"Silent e" Rule**.

- **oa** is in the **middle**

- **ow** and **oe** are at the **end**.

Example Words:

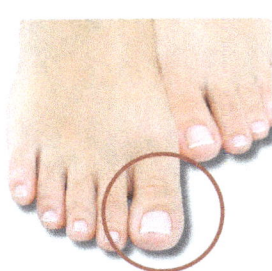

- **oa:** boat, toad

- **oe:** toe, foe

- **ow:** snow, grow

- **o_e:** home, note

LESSON 2.7: Long "u" Vowel Combinations Grouped by Sound: ew, oo, ue, ui, u_e

✏️ **Learner Tip:**

- **oo** is in the **middle.**

- **ue and ew** are at the **end.**

Example Words:

- **ew:** new, chew

- **oo:** moon, food

- **ue:** blue, true

- **ui:** suit, fruit

- **u_e:** flute, cube

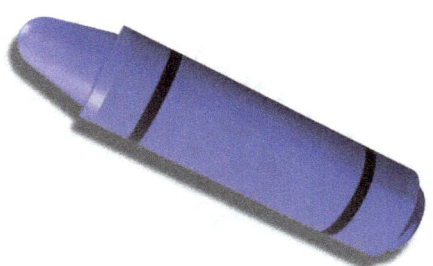

LESSON 2.8: "oi/oy" Vowel Combinations Grouped by Sound

✏️ **Learner Tip:**

- **oi** is in the **middle**

- **oy** is at the **end**.

Example Words:

- **oi:** coin, boil

- **oy:** boy, toy

LESSON 2.9: "ou/ow" Vowel Combinations Grouped by Sound

✏️ **Learner Tip:**

- **ou** often in the **middle**

- **ow** at the **end**.

Example Words:

- **ou:** out, loud

- **ow:** cow, now

LESSON 2.10: "aw" Vowel Combinations Grouped by Sound: al, au, augh, aw/

Example Words:

- **al:** talk, calm

- **au:** author, autumn

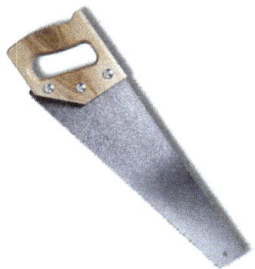

- **augh:** caught

- **aw:** saw, claw

LESSON 2.11: "er" Vowel Combinations Grouped by Sound: er, ear, ir, ur

✏️ **Learner Tip:**

- The "vowel-r" combination blends the harsher "r" sound with the otherwise normal long or short vowel sound into **ir**, or **ur**
- Consider: car, fern, fir.

Example Words:

- er: her
- ear: learn, hear
- ir: bird
- or: work
- ur: turn

LESSON 2.12: Long "a" Words with Vowel Combinations

The long "a" sound is made by the vowel combinations -a, -ai, -ay, and a_e combinations.

Vowel Combination: -a

Example Word	Picture
acorn	
bacon	
ladle	
paper	
potato	

Vowel Combination: -ai

Example Words	Picture
chain	
daisy	
raisin	
snail	
train	

Vowel Combination: -ay

Example Words	Picture
birthd**ay**	
cl**ay**	
gr**ay**	
h**ay**	
tr**ay**	

Vowel Combination: a_e

Example Words	Picture
ape	
face	
mane	
plate	
rake	

Activity 2.1: Long "a" Sound

Directions: Which vowel combinations should we use to create the words below: -ai or -ay?

Example: tr__ __n = tr**ai**n

1. r __ __n
2. st __ __n
3. p __ __n
4. tr __
5. cl __
6. tr __ __n
7. pr __
8. pl __
9. br __ __d
10. t __ __l

LESSON 2.13: Long "e" Words with Vowel Combinations -ea and -ee

The long "e" sound is made by the vowel combinations -ea and -ee.

Vowel Combination: -ea

Example Words	Picture Description	Picture
leak	A faucet with a leak	
eagle	A flying eagle	
leaf	A green leaf	
peach	A juicy peach fruit	
seal	A playful sea animal	

Vowel Combination: -ee

Example Words	Picture Description	Picture
bee	A busy bee	
feet	A pair of feet	
sheep	Two sheep in a field	
steep	A steep cliff	
weeps	A sad woman weeps	

Activity 2.2: Long "e" Sound with -ea and -ee Words

Directions: Select which word describes the picture:

A. peach   B. sheep

A. leaf   B. cheese

A. tree   B. toe

A. seal   B. bee

A. peach   B. leak

A. leaf   B. bee

A. eagle   B. feet

A. seal   B. sheep

A. peach   B. cheese

LESSON 2.14: Long "i" Words with Vowel Combinations -i, -ie, -igh, -y, and i_e

The long "i" sound is made by the vowel combinations -i, -ie, -igh, -y, and i_e.

Vowel Combinations: -i, -ie, -igh, -y, and i_e

Example Words	Picture Description	Picture
bicycle	A bicycle on the sidewalk	
cry	A sad woman began to cry	
dry	A secret spy	
five	The number five	
fly	A buzzing fly	
fry	Fry an egg	
ice	An ice cube	

Example Words	Picture Description	Picture
kite	A colorful flying kite	
knight	A brave knight	
light	A table light	
pie	A pumpkin pie	
slide	A playground slide	

Activity 2.3: Recognizing Long "i" Vowel Combinations

Directions:

- Circle the vowel combination for each long "i" word: -y or i_e.

- Draw a line from each long "i" word to the correct picture.

kite

fry

smile

tie

fly

shy

spy

LESSON 2.15: Long "o" Words with Vowel Combinations -oa, -oe, -ow, and o_e

The long "o" sound is made by the vowel combinations -oa, -oe, -ow, and o_e.

Vowel Combinations: -oa, -oe, -ow, and o_e

Example Words	Picture Description	Picture
boat	A boat on the water	
bone	A dog with a bone	
bow	A ribbon bow	
coat	A warm coat	
cone	An ice cream cone	
goat	A goat on a farm	

Example Word	Picture Description	Picture
Joe	A boy named Joe	
rope	A coiled rope	
snow	Falling snow	
toe	A toe on a foot	

Activity 2.4: Learning the Long "o" Vowel Combination

Directions: Draw a picture of each long "o" vowel combination word in the following phrases:

1. oa   boat   A picture of a boat on the water

2. oa   goat   A playful goat

3. oa   coat   A warm coat hanging on a hanger

4. ow   snow   Snow falling outside

5. ow   window   A window with a snowy scene
                                         outside

6. ow   yellow   A bright yellow hat

7. o_e   rope   A coiled rope

8. o_e   home   A cozy nome

9. o_e   globe   A world globe

10.   oe   toe   A picture of a toe on a foot

Activity 2.5: Understanding the Long "o" Sound-

Directions:

- Underline the long "o" sound in each word.
- Match the word to the picture by drawing a line.

rose

phone

toad

poke

boat

stone

nose

cone

LESSON 2.16: Long "u" Words with Vowel Combinations -u, -u_e, and -oo.

The long "u" sound is made by the vowel combinations -u, -u_e, and -oo.

Vowel Combination: -u

Example Words	Picture Description	Picture
m**u**sic	A piece of sheet music	
uk**u**lele	A man playing a ukulele guitar	
unicorn	A magical unicorn	
unicycles	One-wheeled unicycles	
utensils	Some kitchen tools	

Vowel Combination: u_e

Example Words	Picture Description	Picture
cube	An ice cube	
flute	The flute musical instrument	
June	The month of June	
mule	A mule is similar to a burro	
ruler	A measuring ruler	

Vowel Combination: -oo

Example Words	Picture Description	Picture
broom	A broom to sweep the floor	
cartoon	A cartoon of a silly dinosaur	
pool	A swimming pool	
school	A little red school	
spool	A spool of thread	
spoon	A wooden spoon	
stool	A small, wooden stool	

Example Words	Picture Description	Picture
tatt**oo**	A man with a tattoo	
t**oo**l	A hammer is a type of tool	
t**oo**th	A white tooth	

Activity 2.6: Recognizing Long "u" Vowel Combinations

Directions:

- Circle the "-oo" vowel combination for each long "u" word.
- Draw a line from each long "u" word to the correct picture.

school

tool

pool

tooth

tattoo

spool

spoon

stool

broom

cartoon

Activity 2.7: Practicing Long Vowel Combination Pronunciations with a Partner

Directions: Pronounce more vowel combination words with a partner and then record your voice.

ow	oy	ei	ey
cow	boy	neighbor	alley
gown	royal	vein	honey
howl	employ	leisure	key
power	oyster	sleigh	turkey
ue	**ui**	**ai**	**ay**
blue	cruise	aim	pay
clue	juice	grain	clay
tissue	fluid	hair	spray
statue	penguin	sail	crayon

CHAPTER 3

Short Vowel Combinations

Short vowel combinations in English are typically found in syllables or words where vowel sounds are pronounced quickly and without the tongue gliding.

Formation of the mouth for vowel sounds:

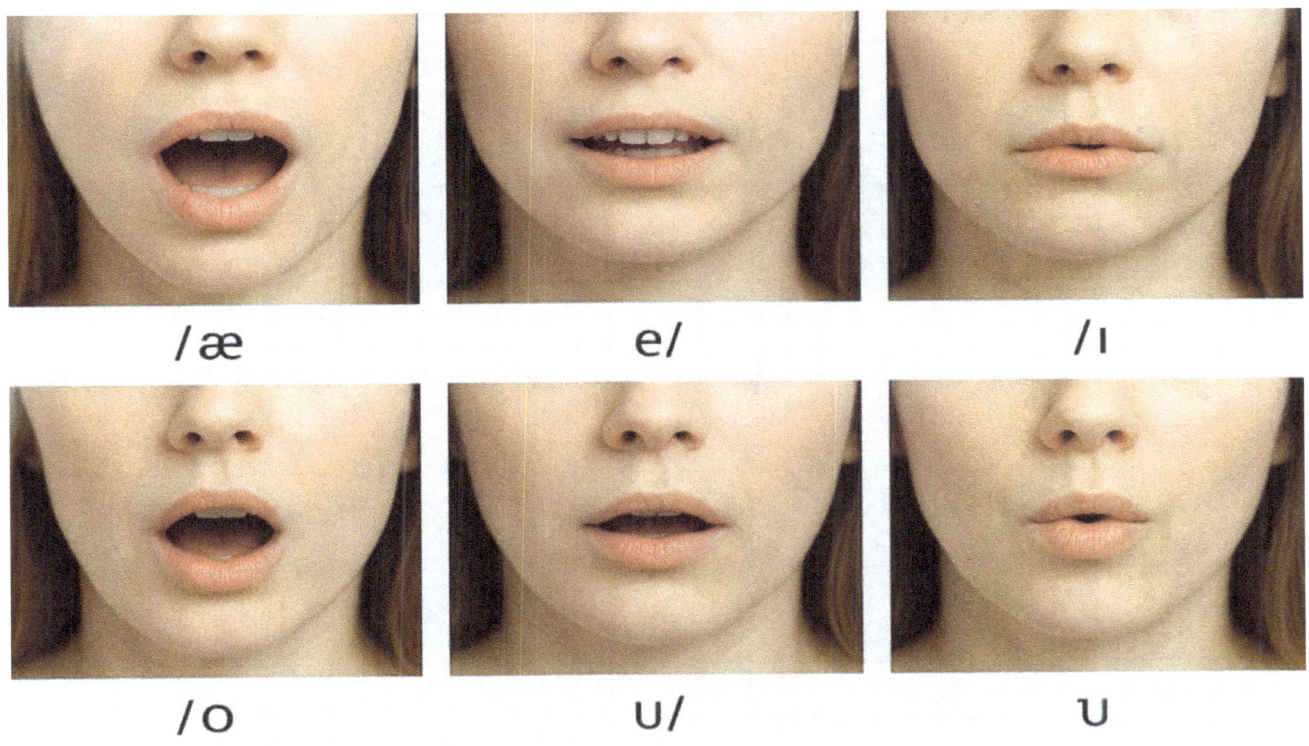

| /æ | e/ | /ɪ |
| /ɒ | ʊ/ | ʊ |

LESSON 3.1: Short Vowel Sounds

Each of the five vowels (a, e, i, o, u) has a short sound as in the examples below:

Short Vowel Sound	Example Words
a	cat, map, bat
e	bed, red, pen
i	sit, bit, ship
o	hot, pot, dog
u	cup, sun, run

The combinations of letters often produce short vowel sounds.

Common Short Vowel Combinations

Combination Sound	Example Words
-ab	cab, grab
-ad	sad, pad
-ed	bed, fed
-ig	pig, big
-op	hop, top
-un	sun, fun
-at	cat, hat

Combination Sound	Example Words
-et	pet, net
-it	sit, fit
-ot	pot, not
-ut	nut, cut

LESSON 3.2: The Short "a" Vowel Sound

Below are some word examples of the short "a" sound with descriptions and pictures:

Word Examples	Picture Descriptions	Picture Ideas
bag	a shopping bag	
hat	A man's hat	
jam	a jar of jam	
map	a folded map	
pan	a frying pan	

Activity 3.1: Practicing the Short "a" Vowel Sound-

Directions: Pronounce these short "a" sound words:

cat   bag

LESSON 3.3: The Short "e" Vowel Sound

Take a closer look at these examples of the short "e" sound with descriptions and picture ideas:

Word Examples	Picture Descriptions	Picture Ideas
bed	a comfy bed for sleep	
bend	a deep forward bend	
hen	a female chicken	
jet	a fast airplane	
web	a spider's web	

Activity 3.2: Practicing the Short "e" Vowel Sound

Directions: Pronounce these short "e" sound words:

bed

legs

LESSON 3.4: The Short "i" Vowel Sound

Below are example words with the short "i" sound with descriptions and pictures:

Word Examples	Picture Descriptions	Picture Ideas
lipstick	Brenda puts on lipstick	
pig	A pig is eating	
pin	A pin holds together a piece of cloth	
sit	Mike likes to sit in a chair	
win	Bob is happy to win a prize	

Activity 3.3: Practicing the Short "i" Sound

Directions: Circle the short "i" word(s) in the phrases below. Use the picture as a reference:

Fish swim in the river

Mary bit into a peach pit

Jack and Jill climbed a hill

The lid on the pot stops a spill

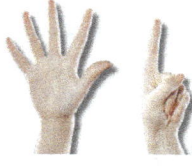

A person holding up six fingers

LESSON 3.5: The Short "o" Vowel Sound

Below are example words with the short "o" sound with descriptions and pictures:

Word Examples	Picture Descriptions	Picture Ideas
box	A container	
dots	A pattern of dots	
frog	A type of toad	
hog	A male pig	
socks	A pair of socks	

Activity 3.4: Practicing the Short "o" Vowel Sound

Directions: Pronounce these short "o" words

moss on rocks

pot

LESSON 3.6: Short "u" Vowel Sound

Below are example words with the short "u" sound with descriptions and pictures:

Word Examples	Picture Descriptions	Picture Ideas
bug	a bug on a leaf	
bus	a school bus	
cup	a cup of tea	
mud	pigs play in the mud	
sun	the sun shines above the clouds	

Activity 3.5: Recognizing the Short "u" Vowel Sound in Words

Directions: Circle the short "u" word in the descriptions below:

Nuts can be a good food

Use scissors to cut paper

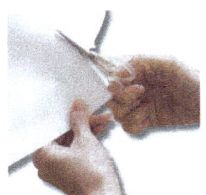

A juicy plum fruit

A pair of mallard ducks

A bear cub with its mother

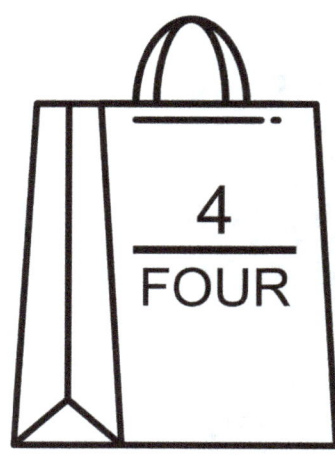

CHAPTER 4

Beginning English Grammar: The Simple Tenses

English uses the simple tense to express basic actions or events. There are three forms of simple tense:

- **Simple Present Tense:** routine or habitual actions, general facts, or events taking place on a fixed schedule

- **Simple Past Tense:** actions or events that have been completed

- **Simple Future Tense:** actions or events that have not happened yet but will at a later time

LESSON 4.1: Present Tense Conjugations of Common English Verbs [Set 1]

The table below lists the first set of present tense conjugations of common English verbs shown for each personal pronoun (I, you, he/she/it, we, they) and the corresponding meanings in Spanish.

Set 1: Present Tense Conjugations of Common English Verbs

English Verb	Subject	English Conjugation	Spanish Translation
be	I	am	yo soy / estoy
	you	are	tú eres / estás
	he/she/it	is	él/ella es / está
	we	are	nosotros(as) somos nosotros(as) estamos
	they	are	ellos(as) son / están
can	I	can	yo puedo
	you	can	tú puedes
	he/she/it	can	él/ella puede
	we	can	nosotros(as) podemos
	they	can	ellos/as pueden
do	I	do	yo hago
	you	do	tú haces
	he/she/it	does	él/ella hace
	we	do	nosotros(as) hacemos
	they	do	ellos(as) hacen
get	I	get	yo obtengo / consigo
	you	get	tú obtienes / consigues
	he/she/it	gets	él/ella obtiene / consigue
	we	get	nosotros(as) obtenemos / conseguimos

English Verb	Subject	English Conjugation	Spanish Translation
	they	get	ellos(as) obtienen / consiguen
go	I	go	yo voy
	you	go	tú vas
	he/she/it	goes	él/ella va
	we	go	nosotros(as) vamos
	they	go	ellos/as van
have	I	have	yo tengo
	you	have	tú tienes
	he/she/it	has	él/ella tiene
	we	have	nosotros(as) tenemos
make	I	make	yo hago / fabrico
	you	make	tú haces / fabricas
	he/she/it	makes	él/ella hace / fabrica
	we	make	nosotros(as) hacemos / fabricamos
	they	make	ellos(as) hacen / fabrican
	they	have	ellos(as) tienen
know	I	know	yo sé / conozco
	you	know	tú sabes / conoces
	he/she/it	knows	él/ella sabe / conoce
	we	know	nosotros(as) sabemos / conocemos

English Verb	Subject	English Conjugation	Spanish Translation
	they	know	ellos(as) saben / conocen
say	I	say	yo digo
	you	say	tú dices
	he/she/it	says	él/ella dice
	we	say	nosotros(as) decimos
	they	say	ellos(as) dicen
think	I	think	yo pienso
	you	think	tú piensas
	he/she/it	thinks	él/ella piensa
	we	think	nosotros(as) pensamos
	they	think	ellos(as) piensan

🖉 **Learner Tip:** For the personal pronouns **I, you, we, or they**, **do not change** the present tense verb.

Examples:

I take a bus. (Yo tomo un autobús.)

You take a bus. (Tú tomas un autobús.)

We take a bus. (Nosotros tomamos un autobús.)

They take a bus. (Ellos toman un autobús.)

🖉 **Learner Tip**: For the personal (third person) pronouns **he, she, and it,** **add an "s" to the end** of the verb.

Examples:

He takes a bus. (Él toma un autobús.)

She takes a bus. (Ella toma un autobús.)

It takes a bus. (Eso toma un autobús.)

🖉 **Learner Tip:** Some verbs (e.g., be, can) are known as "irregular" and do not follow the "s" rule.

Activity 4.1: Present Tense Conjugation with Common Verbs [Set 1]

Directions: Fill in the blank with the correct Present tense form of the verb in parentheses.

Example:

Question: I _____ so happy today.

Answer: I am so happy today.

1. I _____ (be) very tired today.
   (Yo estoy muy cansado hoy.)

2. She _____ (have) two brothers and one sister.
   (Ella tiene dos hermanos y una hermana.)

3. They _____ (do) their homework every afternoon.
   (Ellos hacen su tarea todas las tardes.)

4. He always _____ (say) funny things in class.
   (Siempre dice cosas graciosas en clase.)

5. We _____ (go) to the same school.
   (Nosotros vamos a la misma escuela)

6. You _____ (can) speak three languages!
   (¡Puedes hablar tres idiomas!)

7. She _____ (get) up early on weekdays.
   (Ella se levanta temprano los fines de semana.)

8. I _____ (make) breakfast for my family every morning.
   (Preparo el desayuno para mi familia todas las mañanas.)

9. He _____ (know) the answer to every question.
   (Él sabe la respuesta a todas las preguntas.)

10. They _____ (think) this test is easy.
    (Ellos piensan que esta prueba es fácil.)

Activity 4.2: Oral Questions with Common Present Tense Verbs [Set 1]

Directions:

Answer aloud the questions in the present tense.

Example:

> **Questions: Are** you a hard worker?
>
> **Answer:** Yes, I **am** a hard worker.

1. **Are** you a student? (¿Eres estudiante?)

2. Do they **have** a car? (¿Tienen un coche?)

3. Do you **do** your homework? (¿Haces tu tarea?)

4. What does she **say**? (¿Qué dice ella?)

5. Do we **go** to the same school? (¿Vamos a la misma escuela?)

6. **Can** you swim? (¿Puedes nadar?)

7. Does he **get** a gift every year? (¿Consigue un regalo cada año?)

8. Do you **make** your bed every day? (¿Haces tu cama todos los días?)

9. Do you **know** the answer? (¿Sabes la respuesta?)

10. What do they **think**? (¿Qué piensan ellos?)

LESSON 4.2: More Present Tense Conjugations of Common Verbs Common [Set 2]

Below is a table with the second set of common present tense English verb conjugations. The personal pronoun (I, you, he/she/it, we, they) and its corresponding meaning in Spanish are also shown.

Set 2: Present Tense Conjugations of Common Verbs

English Verb	Subject	English Conjugation	Spanish Translation
call	I	call	yo llamo
	you	call	tú llamas
	he/she/it	calls	él/ella llama
	we	call	nosotros(as) llamamos
	they	call	ellos(as) llaman
come	I	come	yo vengo
	you	come	tú vienes
	he/she/it	comes	él/ella viene
	we	come	nosotros(as) venimos
	they	come	ellos(as) vienen
find	I	find	yo encuentro
	you	find	tú encuentras

English Verb	Subject	English Conjugation	Spanish Translation
	he/she/it	finds	él/ella encuentra
	we	find	nosotros(as) encontramos
	they	find	ellos(as) encuentran
give	I	give	yo doy
	you	give	tú das
	he/she/it	gives	él/ella da
	we	give	nosotros(as) damos
	they	give	ellos(as) dan
see	I	see	yo veo
	you	see	tú ves
	he/she/it	sees	él/ella ve
	we	see	nosotros(as) vemos
	they	see	ellos(as) ven
take	I	take	yo tomo / agarro / llevo
	you	take	tú tomas / agarras / llevas
	he/she/it	takes	él/ella toma / agarra / lleva
	we	take	nosotros(as) tomamos

English Verb	Subject	English Conjugation	Spanish Translation
	they	take	ellos(as) toman
tell	I	tell	yo digo / cuento
	you	tell	tú dices / cuentas
	he/she/it	tells	él/ella dice / cuenta
	we	tell	nosotros/as decimos / contamos
	they	tell	ellos(as) dicen / cuentan
use	I	use	yo uso
	you	use	tú usas
	he/she/it	uses	él/ella usa
	we	use	nosotros(as) usamos
	they	use	ellos(as) usan
want	I	want	yo quiero
	you	want	tú quieres
	he/she/it	wants	él/ella quiere
	we	want	nosotros(as) queremos
	they	want	ellos/as quieren

English Verb	Subject	English Conjugation	Spanish Translation
work	I	work	yo trabajo
	you	work	tú trabajas
	he/she/it	works	él/ella trabaja
	we	work	nosotros(as) trabajamos
	they	work	ellos(as) trabajan

🖉 **Learner Tip:** When answering questions with the personal pronouns **I, you, we, or they,** use the helping verb **"do"**.

Examples:

    I **do** **take** a bus. (Yo tomo un autobús.)

    You **do** **take** a bus. (Tú tomo un autobús.) or (Ustedes toman un autobús.)

    We **do** **take** a bus. (Nosotros tomamos un autobús.)

    They **do** **take** a bus. (Ellos toman un autobús.)

🖉 **Learner Tip**: For the personal third person pronouns **he, she, and it,** use the helping verb **"does"**.

Examples:

    He **does take** a bus. (El toma un autobús.)

    She **does take** a bus. (Ella toma un autobús.)

    It **does take** a bus. (Eso toma un autobús.)

Activity 4.3: Fill in the Blank with Common English Present Tense Verbs (Set 2)

Directions: Fill in the blank with the correct Present tense form of the verb in parentheses.

Example:

>   **Question:** The teacher _____ (tell) us a story every Friday.

>   **Answer:** The teacher **tells** us a story every Friday.

1. He always _____ (take) the bus to school.
   (Él siempre toma el autobús para ir a la escuela)

2. I _____ (see) your point, but I disagree.
   (Entiendo tu punto de vista, pero no estoy de acuerdo.)

3. She _____ (come) to class early every day.
   (Ella viene a clase temprano todos los días.)

4. They _____ (want) to play outside.
   (Ellos quieren jugar afuera.)

5. We _____ (use) this app to study English.
   (Usamos esta aplicación para estudiar inglés.)

6. He often _____ (find) coins on the street.
   (A menudo encuentra monedas en la calle.)

7. I _____ (give) my time to volunteer work.
   (Dedico mi tiempo al trabajo voluntario.)

8. My parents _____ (tell) me to be careful.
   (Mis padres me dicen que tenga cuidado.)

9. She _____ (work) at a hospital.
   (Ella trabaja en el hospital.)

10. You always _____ (call) your grandmother on Sundays.
    (Siempre llamas a tu abuela los domingos.)

Activity 4.4: Oral Questions with Common Present Tense Verbs (Set 2)

Directions: Answer aloud the questions below using the Present tense verbs **(in bold) + do/does.**

Example:

> **Question:** Does she **work** here?
>
> **Answer:** Yes, **she does** work here.

1. Do **I take** this book? (¿Tomo este libro?)

2. Does **she take** the keys? (Toma ella las llaves?)

3. Do **we take** our lunch? (¿Tomamos nuestro almuerzo?)

4. Do **they take** pictures? (¿Toman ellos fotos?)

5. Do **I see** the problem? (¿Veo el problema?)

6. Do **you see** the stars? (¿Ves las estrellas?)

7. Does **he see** the cat? (¿Ve él al gato?)

8. Do **they see** us? (¿Nos ven ellos?)

9. Do **I come** on time? (¿Vengo a tiempo?)

10. Do **you come** every day? (¿Vienes todos los días?)

LESSON 4.3: Common Simple Past Tense Verbs

Most Past tense verbs in English are formed by **adding -d or -ed** to the verb.

Use the table below to become more familiar with simple Past tense verbs.

Common Simple Past Tense Verbs

English Verb	English Past Tense Example	Spanish Verb	Spanish Past Tense Example
ask	I ask**ed**	preguntar	Yo pregunté
call	I call**ed**	llamar	Yo llamé
clean	I clean**ed**	limpiar	Yo limpié
close	I clos**ed**	cerrar	Yo cerré
cook	I cook**ed**	cocinar	Yo cociné
decide	I decid**ed**	decidir	Yo decidí
dress	I dress**ed**	vestirse	Yo me vestí
explain	I explain**ed**	explicar	Yo expliqué
finish	I finish**ed**	terminar	Yo terminé
help	I help**ed**	ayudar	Yo ayudé
jump	I jump**ed**	saltar	Yo salté
listen	I listen**ed**	escuchar	Yo escuché
live	I liv**ed**	vivir	Yo viví
look	I look**ed**	mirar	Yo miré
love	I lov**ed**	amar	Yo amé
open	I open**ed**	abrir	Yo abrí

English Verb	English Past Tense Example	Spanish Verb	Spanish Past Tense Example
play	I play**ed**	jugar	Yo jugué
start	I start**ed**	empezar	Yo empecé
talk	I talk**ed**	hablar	Yo hablé
travel	I travel**ed**	viajar	Yo viajé
use	I use**d**	usar	Yo usé
walk	I walk**ed**	caminar	Yo caminé
watch	I watch**ed**	ver	Yo vi
work	I work**ed**	trabajar	Yo trabajé

LESSON 4.4: Common Irregular Past Tense Verbs

English irregular Past tense verbs often **do not follow the rule** of adding "-d" or "-ed" to the end of the simple verb.

Below are examples of common irregular Past tense English verbs, with the present tense verb in parentheses:

Common Irregular Past Tense Verbs

English Verb (Past Tense)	English Past Tense Example	Spanish Verb	Spanish Past Tense Example
be (was/were)	I **was** happy. We **were** happy.	ser / estar (fui/fue/estuve)	Yo fui feliz. Yo estuve feliz.
buy (bought)	He **bought** a car.	comprar (compré)	Él compró un coche.
come (came)	He **came** to the party.	venir (vine)	Él vino a la fiesta.
drink (drank)	I **drank** water.	bebí (beber)	Yo bebí agua.
drop (dropped)	I **dropped**	dejé caer (dejar caer)	Yo dejé caer
eat (ate)	I **ate** lunch.	comer (comí)	Yo comí almuerzo.
find (found)	He **found** his keys.	encontrar (encontré)	Él encontró sus llaves
go (went)	She **went** to the store.	ir (fui)	Ella fue a la tienda.
have (had)	I **had** a car.	tener (tuve)	Yo tuve un coche.

English Verb (Past Tense)	English Past Tense Example	Spanish Verb	Spanish Past Tense Example
know (knew)	We **knew** the answer.	saber (supe)	Nosotros supimos la respuesta.
make (made)	She **made** a cake.	hacer (hice)	Ella hizo un pastel.
plan (planned)	I **planned**	planeé (planear)	Yo planeé
read [long "e"] read [short "e"]	She **read** a book.	leer (leí)	Ella leyó un libro.
run (ran)	We **ran** in the park.	correr (corrí)	Nosotros corrimos en el parque.
see (saw)	We **saw** a movie.	ver (vi)	Nosotros vimos una película.
sing (sang)	She **sang** in a rock band.	cantar (canté)	Ella canté una bande de rock.
sleep (slept)	They **slept** all night.	dormir (dormí)	Ellos durmieron toda la noche.
speak (spoke)	He **spoke** Spanish.	hablar (hablé)	Él habló español.
take (took)	I **took** a picture.	tomar (tomé)	Yo tomé una foto.
try (tried)	I **tried**	intenté (intentar)	Yo intenté
understand (understood)	I **understood** the lesson.	entender (entendí)	Yo entendí la lección.
write (wrote)	They **wrote** a letter.	escribir (escribí)	Ellos escribieron una carta.

✏ Learner Tip:

- In Spanish, -é is added to -ar verbs (e.g., trabajar = trabajé). Verbs ending in -er, -ir, and -í are added to the end (e.g., beber = bebí; dormir = dormí).

- **Regular Verbs:** Follow a predictable pattern in the Past tense. In English, -ed is generally added to the end of the verb (e.g., play = played).

- **Irregular Verbs:** These verbs do not follow a predictable pattern in either English or Spanish. Each form must be memorized (e.g., to go = went; ir = fui).

Activity 4.5: Fill in the Blank with Past Tense Verbs

Directions: Complete the sentences using the Past tense verb in parentheses, either simple (regular) or irregular.

Example:

> **Questions:** She _____ (go) to the store yesterday.

> **Answer: She went** to the store yesterday.
> ("Go" is an irregular verb; the Past Simple is "went.")

1. I _____ (eat) pizza for dinner last night.
   (Anoche cené pizza.)

2. I _____ (be) at the library yesterday.
   (Anoche estuve en la biblioteca.)

3. They _____ (work) until midnight.
   (Ellos trabajaron hasta la medianoche.)

4. She _____ (have) a cold last week.
   (Ella tuvo un resfriado la semana pasada)

5. We _____ (play) soccer after school.
   (Nosotros jugamos fútbol despues de la escuela.)

6. He _____ (make) a big mistake.
   (Cometió un gran error.)

7. You _____ (call) me yesterday, right?
   (Me llamaste ayer, ¿verdad?)

8. I _____ (see) that movie last month.
   (Vi esa película el mes pasado.)

9. The children _____ (watch) a cartoon.
   (Los niños vieron una caricatura)

10. My mom _____ (buy) some new shoes.
    (Mi madre compró zapatos nuevos.)

Activity 4.6: Oral Answers with Past Tense Verbs

Directions: Answer aloud these questions with the proper Past tense verb.

Example:

Question: What did you **make** for breakfast this morning?

Answer: I made pancakes and scrambled eggs for breakfast this morning.

1. What did you do yesterday?
   (¿Qué hiciste ayer?)

2. Did you travel anywhere last summer?
   (¿Viajaste a algún lugar el verano pasado?)

3. Who did you meet at the party?
   (¿A quién conociste en la fiesta?)

4. Did you watch the movie last night?
   (¿Viste la película anoche?)

5. Where did you grow up?
   (¿Dónde creciste?)

6. Did you have breakfast this morning?
   (¿Desayunaste esta mañana?)

7. What time did you go to bed last night?
   (¿A qué hora te acostaste anoche?)

8. Did you study for the exam?
   (¿Estudiaste para el examen?)

9. How did you celebrate your last birthday?
   (¿Cómo celebraste tu último cumpleaños?)

10. Did you call your family yesterday?
    (¿Llamaste a tu familia ayer?)

LESSON 4.5: The Simple Future Tense

In English, the Future tense is commonly formed by using **"will"** or **"going to"** (for plans or intentions). In Spanish, the Future tense is conjugated directly into the verb itself without any auxiliary verb.

🖊 **Learner Tip:**

- "Will" is used for predictions, promises, offers, and general future actions (e.g., I will call you) that are certain to happen.

- "Going to" is often used for plans or intentions that are already decided before the moment of speaking (e.g., I am going to eat dinner).

Example:

She **will visit** us next week. (Ella nos **visitará** la próxima semana.)

Future Tense Conjugations

Subject	English (Future)	Spanish (Futuro)
I	will + verb am going to + verb	infinitive + é
You	will + verb are going to + verb	infinitive + ás
He/She/It	will + verb is going to + verb	infinitive + á
We	will + verb are going to + verb	infinitive + emos
They	will + verb are going to + verb	infinitive + án

Common Future Tense Verb Conjugations

Subject	English	Spanish
I	I **will go** to the store. **I am going to go** to the store.	Yo iré a la tienda.
You	You **will study** hard. You **are going to study** hard.	Tú estudiarás mucho.
He/She/It	She **will eat** pizza. She **is going to eat** pizza.	Ella comerá pizza.
We	We **will travel** next year. **We are going to travel** next year.	Nosotros viajaremos el próximo año.
They	They **will finish** the project. They **are going to finish** the project.	Ellos terminarán el proyecto.

Activity 4.7: Fill in the Blank Using the Future Tense

Directions: Answer each question with the correct form of the Future tense verb in parentheses.

Examples:

We will watch a movie.

We are going to watch a movie.

1. I _____ (work) late tomorrow.
   (Trabajaré hasta tarde mañana.)

2. She _____ (play) soccer with her friends on Saturday.
   (Ella jugará al fútbol con sus amigas el sábado.)

3. They _____ (watch) a movie tonight.
   (Ellos verán una película esta noche.)

4. We _____ (call) you as soon as we arrive.
   (Te llamaremos tan pronto como lleguemos.)

5. He _____ (help) you with your homework.
   (Él te ayudará con tu tarea.)

Activity 4.8: Oral Answers Using the Future Tense

Directions: Answer aloud each question with the correct form of the Future tense form of "going to" + verb.

Example:

Question: Will you go to the dance on Saturday?

Answer: Yes, I will go to the dance on Saturday.

1. What will you do this weekend?
   (¿Qué harás este fin de semana?)

2. Will you travel somewhere next year?
   (¿Viajarás a algún lugar el próximo año?)

3. Will you study a new language in the future?
   (¿Estudiarás un nuevo idioma en el futuro?)

4. When will you start your new job?
   (¿Cuándo empezarás tu nuevo trabajo?)

5. Will you celebrate your birthday with friends?
   (¿Celebrarás tu cumpleaños con amigos?)

Activity 4.9: Oral Answers Using the Future Tense with Different Subjects

Directions: Answer aloud each question with the correct form of the Future tense combination of "will/will not" + verb.

Example:

> **Question:** Will Mark and Rosa attend the soccer game on Friday night?

> **Answer:** No, Mark and Rosa will not attend the soccer game on Friday night because they are both sick.

1. Will I see you tomorrow?
   (¿Me veré contigo mañana?)

2. Will you come to the party?
   (¿Vendrás a la fiesta?)

3. Will he start a new job soon?
   (¿Él empezará un nuevo trabajo pronto?)

4. Will she travel abroad next year?
   (¿Ella viajará al extranjero el próximo año?)

5. Will it be sunny this weekend?
   (¿Estará soleado este fin de semana?)

6. Will we meet at the café later?
   (¿Nos encontraremos en el café más tarde?)

7. Will they join us for dinner?
   (¿Ellos se unirán a nosotros para cenar?)

Activity 4.10: Fill in the Blank with the Future Tense Combination "going to"

Directions: Complete the sentences using the correct form of "going to" + verb.

Example:

> **Question:** Are you going to go to the picnic?

> **Answer:** Yes, I am going to the picnic.

1. I _____ _____ (visit) my grandmother this weekend.
   (Voy a visitar a mi abuela este fin de semana.)

2. She _____ _____ (study) for the math test tonight.
   (Ella va a estudiar para el examen de matemáticas esta noche.)

3. They _____ _____ (cook) dinner together.
   (Ellos van a cocinar la cena juntos.)

4. We _____ _____ (travel) to Spain next summer.
   (Vamos a viajar a España el próximo verano.)

5. He _____ _____ (clean) his room after school.
   (Él va a limpiar su cuarto después de la escuela.)

Activity 4.11: Oral Answers Using Future Tense Combination "going to"

Directions: Answer aloud each question with the correct form of the Future tense combination of "going to" + verb.

Example:

Question: Are you going to go swimming this afternoon?

Answer: No, I am not going to go swimming this afternoon because it is too cold.

1. Are you going to travel this summer?
   (¿Vas a viajar este verano?)

2. What are you going to do after work today?
   (¿Qué vas a hacer después del trabajo hoy?)

3. Is she going to start a new hobby?
   (¿Ella va a empezar un nuevo pasatiempo?)

4. Are we going to meet later this week?
   (¿Vamos a reunirnos más tarde esta semana?)

5. Are they going to move to a new city?
   (¿Ellos van a mudarse a una nueva ciudad?)

Activity 4.12: Oral Answers Using Future Tense combination "going to" with Different Subjects

Directions: Answer aloud each question with the correct form of the Future tense combination of "going to" + verb.

Example:
> **Question:** Is Rebecca going to visit her grandmother in Peru this summer?

> **Answer:** Yes, Rebecca is going to visit her grandmother in Peru this summer.

1. Am I going to see you at the party?
   (¿Voy a verte en la fiesta?)

2. Are you going to study tonight?
   (¿Vas a estudiar esta noche?)

3. Is he going to call you later?
   (¿Él va a llamarte más tarde?)

4. Is she going to visit her family soon?
   (¿Ella va a visitar a su familia pronto?)

5. Is it going to rain tomorrow?
   (¿Va a llover mañana?)

6. Are we going to have dinner together?
   (¿Vamos a cenar juntos?)

7. Are they going to start the project next week?
   (¿Ellos van a empezar el proyecto la próxima semana?)

LESSON 4.6: Common Irregular Verbs in the Future Tense

In English, Future tense verbs do not change with the subject **but are preceded by "will" or "going to"**. In Spanish, however, some verbs have irregular stems in the Future tense, but the endings remain the same.

The verb "can" is a special case. The Future tense becomes 'be able to'.

Common Irregular Future Tense Verb Conjugations

English Verb	Future Tense English Example	Spanish Irregular Verb	Spanish Irregular Stem	Spanish Example
can (be able to)	will be able to	poder	podr-	Tú podrás
do	will do	hacer	har-	Nosotros haremos
have (state of being)	there will be__	haber	habr-	Habrá
have (possession)	will have	tener	tendr-	Ellos tendrán
say	will say	decir	dir-	Yo diré

Activity 4.13: Fill in the Blank with Future Tense Irregular Verbs

Directions: Complete the sentences using the correct simple Future tense form of the verb in parentheses. Use **will + base form** of the verb. For the verb "**can**," use "**will be able to**".

1. I _____ (say) something nice to her later.
   (Diré algo amable más tarde.)

2. He _____ (tell) you the story tomorrow.
   (Él te contará la historia mañana.)

3. We _____ (have) more time next week.
(Tendremos más tiempo la próxima semana.)

4. They _____ (can) solve the problem soon.
(Podrán resolver el problema pronto.)

5. She _____ (come) to the meeting at 3 p.m.
(Ella vendrá a la reunión a las 3 p.m.)

Activity 4.14: Oral Answers Using Irregular Verbs in the Future Tense

Directions: Answer aloud each question with the correct form of the Future tense irregular verb.

Example:

> **Question:** Will she take the test next week?
>
> **Answer:** No, she will not take the test because it was postponed.

1. Will you go to the concert next week?
(¿Irás al concierto la próxima semana?)

2. Will she have time to help us?
(¿Tendrá ella tiempo para ayudarnos?)

3. Will they see the new movie soon?
(¿Verán ellos la nueva película pronto?)

4. Will he make a decision today?
(¿Tomará él una decisión hoy?)

5. Will we know the results by tomorrow?
(¿Sabremos los resultados para mañana?)

Activity 4.15: Oral Answers Using Irregular Verbs in the Future Tense with Different Subjects

Directions: Answer aloud each question with the correct form of the Future tense irregular verb.

Example:

> **Question:** Will you go to the concert tomorrow?
>
> **Answer:** Yes, I will go to the concert with my friends.

1. Will I go to the meeting tomorrow?
   (¿Iré a la reunión mañana?)

2. Will you have lunch with me?
   (¿Almorzarás conmigo?)

3. Will he see his family next month?
   (¿Él verá a su familia el próximo mes?)

4. Will she make a cake for the party?
   (¿Ella hará un pastel para la fiesta?)

5. Will it be cold tonight?

   (¿Hará frío esta noche?)

6. Will we know the answer soon?
   (¿Sabramos la respuesta pronto?)

7. Will they take the bus to school?
   (¿Ellos tomarán el autobús a la escuela?)

CHAPTER 5

Intermediate English Grammar: The Progressive Tenses

Progressive tenses (also called continuous tenses) in English describe ongoing or unfinished actions in the past, present, or future. They are created with a form of "to be" plus the present participle of the base verb (the "-ing" form).

LESSON 5.1: The Present Progressive Tense

The Present Progressive tense (also called the Present Continuous tense) in English is used to describe **actions that are happening right now or temporary actions**. It is formed with the **verb "to be"** in the present tense and the **"-ing"** form of the main verb.

For comparison, the Present Progressive in Spanish is formed with the verb "estar" in the Present tense and the endings "-ando" for "-ar" verbs or "-iendo" for "-er" and "-ir" verbs.

Present Progressive Conjugations of Common Verbs

Subject	English Present Progressive	Spanish Present Progressive	English Example	Spanish Example
I	**am** + verb-**ing**	estoy + verb -ando / -iendo	I am eating.	Yo estoy comiendo.
You	**are** + verb-**ing**	estás + verb -ando / -iendo	You are studying.	Tú estás estudiando.
He/She/It	**is** + verb-**ing**	está + verb -ando / -iendo	She is reading.	Ella está leyendo.
We	**are** + verb-**ing**	estamos + verb -ando / -iendo	We are working.	Nosotros estamos trabajando.
They	**are** + verb-**ing**	están + verb -ando / -iendo	They are traveling.	Ellos están viajando.

🖉 **Learner Tip**:

- For "**-ar**" **verbs**: use "**-ando**" (e.g., **hablar → hablando**)
- For "**-er**" and "**-ir**" **verbs**: use "**-iendo**" (e.g., **comer → comiendo**; **vivir → viviendo**)
- The Present Progressive emphasizes that the action is ongoing or in progress right now (at the moment).

Activity 5.1: Practicing the Present Progressive Tense

Directions: Fill in the blanks using the Present Progressive form of the verbs in parentheses.

Example:

> **Question:** Pamela (looks) at a bear in the woods
>
> **Answer:** Pamela **is looking** at a bear in the woods.

1. She _____ _____ a very interesting book right now.
     (to be)   (read)

2. We _____ _____ a movie at the cinema.
     (to be)   (watch)

3. I _____ _____ dinner for my family.
    (to be)   (cook)

4. They _____ soccer in the park.
       (to be)   (play)

5. He _____ _____ for his math exam.
     (to be)   (study)

6. You _____ _____ to music too loudly.
      (to be)   (listen)

7. The baby _____ _____ in her crib.
          (to be)   (sleep)

8. What _____ you _____ at the moment?
       (to be)   (do)

9. _____ she _____ on the new project?
    (to be)   (work)

10. Why _____ they _____ (run) so fast?
         (to be)   (run)

Activity 5.2: Oral Questions with the Present Progressive Tense

Directions: Answer aloud the personal questions below using the Present Progressive in English.

Example:

Question: What are you watching on television?

Answer: I am watching the Discovery Channel.

1. What are you doing right now?
(¿Que estás haciendo en este momento?)

2. Are you working on any projects at the moment?
(¿Estás trabajando en algún proyecto en este momento?)

3. Are you living with your family or on your own?
(¿Vives con tu familia o solo/a?)

4. Are you studying anything new these days?
(¿Estás estudiando algo nuevo últimamente?)

5. Are you planning a vacation this year?
(¿Estás planeando unas vacaciones este año?)

Activity 5.3: Oral Questions with the Present Progressive Tense and Different Subjects

Directions: Answer aloud the questions below using the Present

Progressive tense with different subjects:

Example:

> **Question:** What are your friends doing on Friday?

> **Answer:** My friends are drawing pictures for their class project on
>   Friday.

1. What are you doing this weekend? (you)
(¿Qué vas a hacer este fin de semana?)

2. Is she studying for her exams right now? (she)
(¿Está estudiando para sus exámenes ahora mismo?)

3. Are they watching a movie at the moment? (they)
(¿Están viendo una película en este momento?)

4. What is he cooking for dinner? (he)
(¿Qué está cocinando para la cena?)

5. Are we meeting them later today? (we)
(¿Nos reuniremos con ellos más tarde hoy?

6. Is it raining outside? (it)
(¿Está lloviendo afuera?)

7. Am I speaking too fast? (I)
(¿Estoy hablando demasiado rápido?)

LESSON 5.2: The Past Progressive Tense

The Past Progressive tense (also known as the Past Continuous tense) is used to describe an **action that was ongoing or in progress at a specific time in the past**. It often sets the background for another event or shows two actions happening at the same time. It is formed by **was/were + present verb.**

✏️ **Learner Tip:**

- I/he/she/it → **was** + verb-ing
- You/we/they → **were** + verb-ing **participle (verb + -ing)**

Example:

They _____ (watch) TV when the phone rang.

They were watching TV <u>when</u> the phone rang.

(The action "watching TV" was in progress when another action happened.)

Common Verbs with Past Progressive Conjugations

English Verb	Past Progressive (I/He/She/It)	Past Progressive (They/We)	Spanish (Past Progressive)
come	**was** com**ing**	**were** com**ing**	estaba / estaban viniendo
do	**was** do**ing**	**were** do**ing**	estaba / estaban haciendo
eat	**was** eat**ing**	**were** eat**ing**	estaba / estaban comiendo
go	**was** go**ing**	**were** go**ing**	estaba / estaban yendo

English Verb	Past Progressive (I/He/She/It)	Past Progressive (They/We)	Spanish (Past Progressive)
have	**was** hav**ing**	**were** hav**ing**	estaba / estaban teniendo
make	**was** mak**ing**	**were** mak**ing**	estaba / estaban haciendo
read	**was** read**ing**	**were** read**ing**	estaba / estaban leyendo
write	**was** writ**ing**	**were** writ**ing**	estaba / estaban escribiendo

Activity 5.4: Fill in the Blank with the Past Progressive Tense

Directions: Complete the sentences using the Past Progressive form of the verb in parentheses.

Examples:

She **was reading** a book when I called her.

They **were eating** (eat) dinner when the doorbell rang.

1. They _____ (go) to the park while it was raining.
   (Ellos estaban yendo al parque mientras estaba lloviendo)

2. We _____ (do) our homework at 7 p.m. yesterday.
   (Estábamos haciendo nuestros deberes a las 7:00 de la tarde de ayer.)

3. He _____ (have) a meeting when I arrived.
   (Estaba en una reunión cuando llegué.)

4. You _____ (make) a lot of noise last night.
   (Estabas haciendo mucho ruido anoche.)

5. She _____ (come) to the party when I saw her.
   (Ella venía a la fiesta cuando la vi.)

6. The children _____ (write) stories in class.
   (Los niños estaban escribiendo historias en clase.)

7. My parents _____ (read) the newspaper in the morning.
   (Mis padres estaban leyendo el periódico por la mañana.)

Activity 5.5: Oral Answers Using the Past Progressive Tense

Directions: Answer aloud the following questions using the correct Past Progressive verb.

Example:

> **Question:** What **were you doing** <u>when</u> the power went out?
>
> **Answer: I was watching** a movie <u>when</u> the power went out.

1. What were you doing at 8 p.m. last night?
   (¿Qué estabas haciendo a las 8 p.m. anoche?)

2. Was she working when you called?
   (¿Ella estaba trabajando cuando llamaste?)

3. Were they playing soccer when it started to rain?
   (¿Ellos estaban jugando fútbol cuando empezó a llover?)

4. Who were you talking to on the phone?
   (¿Con quién estabas hablando por teléfono?)

5. Were we waiting long before the bus arrived?
   (¿Estuvimos esperando mucho antes de que llegara el autobús?)

LESSON 5.3: The Future Progressive Tense

The Future Progressive tense (also known as the Future Continuous tense) describes an **action that will be in progress at a specific time in the future**. It often indicates that something will be happening at a particular moment.

🖉 **Learner Tip:** The Future Progressive Tense is formed by:

- will be + present participle (verb + -ing)

Example:

This time tomorrow, **I will be working** at the office.

(The action "working" will be ongoing at a specific future time.)

Common Verb Conjugations in Future Progressive Tense

English Verb	Future Progressive Example	Spanish Translation
call	We **will be** call**ing**.	Nosotros estaremos llamando.
cook	You **will be** cook**ing**.	Tu estarás cocinando.
play	She **will be** play**ing**.	Ella estará jugando.
read	You **will be** read**ing**.	Ustedes estarán leyendo.
study	They **will be** study**ing**.	Ellos estudiaran
travel	I **will be** travel**ing**.	Estaré viajando.
watch	He **will be** watch**ing**.	Él estará mirando.
work	I **will be** work**ing**.	Estaré trabajando.

Activity 5.6: Fill in the Blank with Future Progressive Verbs

Directions: Complete the sentences using the Future Progressive form of the verb in parentheses.

Example:

> **Question:** At 8 p.m. tonight, she _____ (study) for her exam
>
> **Answer:** At 8 p.m. tonight, **she will be studying** for her exam.

1. Tomorrow at noon, I _____ (work) on the report.

2. Next Friday, they _____ (play) in the soccer match.

3. At this time tomorrow, we _____ (watch) a movie.

4. She _____ (call) you later tonight.

5. He _____ (study) all weekend for the test.

6. We _____ (cook) dinner when you arrive.

7. They _____ (travel) to New York next week.

8. I _____ (read) the new book tomorrow evening.

Activity 5.7: Oral Answers Using the Future Progressive Tense

Directions: Answer aloud each question with the correct form of the Future Progressive tense.

Example:

> **Question:** How long will you have been studying English by the end of this year?
>
> **Answer:** I will have been studying English for six years by the end of this year.

1. What will you be doing this weekend?
   (¿Qué estarás haciendo este fin de semana?)

2. Will you be working late tonight?
   (¿Estarás trabajando hasta tarde esta noche?)

3. Will she be traveling next month?
   (¿Estará ella viajando el próximo mes?)

4. Will we be meeting at the café tomorrow?
   (¿Nos estaremos reuniendo en el café mañana?)

5. Will they be watching the game on TV?
   (¿Estarán ellos viendo el partido en la televisión?)

Activity 5.8: Oral Answers Using the Future Progressive Tense with Different Subjects

Directions: Answer aloud each question with the correct form of the Future Progressive tense verb.

Example:

> **Question:** How long will Eric have been working in the United States by the end of this year?
>
> **Answer:** Eric will have been working in the United States for 15 years by the end of this year.

1. Will I be joining the meeting later?
   (¿Estaré yo uniéndome a la reunión más tarde?)

2. Will you be working from home tomorrow?
   (¿Estarás trabajando desde casa mañana?)

3. Will he be studying for the exam this weekend?
   (¿Estará él estudiando para el examen este fin de semana?)

4. Will she be cooking dinner when I arrive?
   (¿Estará ella cocinando la cena cuando llegué?)

5. Will it be raining during the afternoon?
   (¿Estará lloviendo durante la tarde?)

6. Will we be traveling together next month?
   (¿Estaremos viajando juntos el próximo mes?)

7. Will they be waiting for us at the airport?
   (¿Estarán ellos esperándonos en el aeropuerto?)

CHAPTER 6

Intermediate English Grammar: The Perfect Tenses

LESSON 6.1: The Present Perfect Tense

Present Perfect tenses in English are formed with **have (have/has/had) + past participle**. In Spanish, Present Perfect tenses are formed with **haber (he/has/ha/había/habrá) + past participle**.

The Present Perfect tense is used to describe actions or events **that have occurred sometime in the past and are still relevant to the present** or were **started in the past and continue into the present**.

✏️ **Learner Tip:**
- Use **have** with I/you/we/they
- Use **has** with he/she/it

Examples:

    English: eat → ate → eaten = I have eaten lunch

    Spanish: comer → comí → comido = He comido almuerzo

Common English Verbs in the Present Perfect Tense

English Verb	English Present Perfect	Spanish
be	have/has **been**	he/ha **sido / estado**
do	have/has **done**	he/ha **hecho**
get	have/has **gotten**	he/ha **obtenido / conseguido**
go	have/has **gone**	he/ha **ido**
have	have/has **had**	he/ha **tenido**
know	have/has **known**	he/ha **sabido / conocido**
make	have/has **made**	he/ha **hecho**
say	have/has **said**	he/ha **dicho**
take	have/has **taken**	he/ha **tomado / llevado**
think	have/has **thought**	he/ha **pensado**

Activity 6.1: Present Perfect Tense Fill in the Blank

Directions: Complete the sentences with the correct Present Perfect form of the verb in parentheses.

Example:

   Question: My brother _____ _____ breakfast already.

   Answer: My brother **has eaten** breakfast already.

1. I _____ _____ (be) to New York twice.

2. She _____ _____ (have) a lot of work lately.

3. They _____ _____ (do) all their homework.

4. We _____ _____ (say) that many times.

5. He _____ _____ (go) to the store.

6. You _____ _____ (get) a promotion, right?

7. She _____ _____ (make) a beautiful painting.

8. I _____ _____ (know) her since we were kids.

9. They _____ _____ (think) about changing jobs.

10. We _____ _____ (take) that test already.

Activity 6.2: Present Perfect Tense Oral Answers

Directions: Respond aloud to each question with: "Yes, I have done _____"

or "No I have not (haven't) done _____."

Example:

Question: Have you ever hiked Mount Everest?

Answer: No, I have not hiked Mount Everest.

1. Have you ever traveled to another country?
   (¿Has viajado alguna vez a otro país?)

2. Have you finished your homework yet?
   (¿Ya has terminado tu tarea?)

3. Have you tried sushi before?
   (¿Has probado el sushi antes?)

4. Have you lived in your home a long time?
(¿Has vivido tú en tu casa durante mucho tiempo?)

5. Have you seen that new movie yet?
(¿Ya has visto esa nueva película?)

Activity 6.3: Present Perfect Tense Oral Answers with Different Subjects

Directions: Respond aloud to each question with the proper form of the Present Perfect Tense verb.

Example:

Question: Has your mother ever lived in San Jose, Costa Rica?

Answer: Yes, my mother has lived in San Jose, Costa Rica.

1. Have **you** ever met a famous person?
(¿Alguna vez has conocido a una persona famosa?)

2. Has **she** finished her project?
(¿Ella ha terminado su proyecto?)

3. Have **they** visited this museum before?
(¿Ellos han visitado este museo antes?)

4. Has **he** ever cooked dinner for you?
(¿Él ha cocinado la cena para ti alguna vez?)

5. Have **we** done everything we need to do?
(¿Hemos hecho todo lo que necesitamos que hacer?)

LESSON 6.2: The Past Perfect Tense

The Past Perfect Tense is used to describe an action that was completed before another action or time in the past. It is formed by **had + past participle of the verb**. The auxiliary "had" is used for all subjects.

Example:

I **had eaten** dinner <u>before</u> they arrived.

(The eating happened before "they arrived")

Common Verbs in the Past Perfect Tense

English Verb	English Past Perfect	Spanish Past Perfect
be	**had** been	había sido
come	**had** come	había venido
do	**had** done	había hecho
give	**had** given	había dado
go	**had** gone	había ido
make	**had** made	había hecho
see	**had** seen	había visto
take	**had** taken	había tomado / llevado

Activity 6.4: Fill in the Blank with the Past Perfect Tense

Directions: Complete the sentences using the Past Perfect form of the verb in parentheses.

Example:

> **Question:** She _____ _____ (go) to the store before it started raining.
> **Answer:** She **had gone** to the store <u>before</u> it started raining.

1. I _____ (see) the movie before you told me about it.
   (Ella había ido a la tienda antes de que empezara a llover.)

2. They _____ (do) all their homework before dinner.
   (Habían hecho todos sus deberes antes de la cena.)

3. We _____ (have) enough food for everyone.
   (Habíamos tenido suficiente comida para todos. amos tenido suficiente comida para todos.)

4. He _____ (make) a reservation before arriving.
   (Había hecho una reservación antes de llegar.)

5. You _____ (come) to the meeting too early.
   (Habías llegado a la reunión demasiado temprano.)

6. She _____ (take) the test before the others arrived.
   (Ella había tomado la prueba antes de que llegaran las demás.)

Activity 6.5: Oral Answers with the Past Perfect Tense

Directions: Answer aloud the sentences using the Past Perfect form of the verb in parentheses.

Example:

> **Question:** What **had you done** <u>before</u> the guests arrived?
>
> **Answer: I had cleaned** the house and **prepared** dinner <u>before</u> the guests arrived.

1. Had you finished your homework before dinner?
   (¿Habías terminado tu tarea antes de la cena?)

2. Had she already left when you arrived?
   (¿Ella ya se había ido cuando llegaste?)

3. Had they traveled abroad before last year?
   (¿Habían viajado al extranjero antes del año pasado?)

4. Had he studied English before moving to the United States?
   (¿Había estudiado inglés antes de mudarse a Estados Unidos?)

5. Had we met before the party?
   (¿Nos habíamos conocido antes de la fiesta?)

Activity 6.6: Oral Answers Using the Past Perfect Tense with Different Subjects

Directions: Answer aloud the sentences with different subjects using the Past Perfect form of the verb in parentheses

Example:

> **Question:** What **had he done** <u>before</u> he took out the garbage?
>
> **Answer: He had walked** the dog <u>before</u> he took out the garbage.

1. Had you already eaten when I called?
   (¿Ya habías comido cuando llamé?)

2. Had she finished her work before the meeting started?
   (¿Ella había terminado su trabajo antes de que empezara la reunión?)

3. Had they visited that city before their last trip?
   (¿Ellos habían visitado esa ciudad antes de su último viaje?)

4. Had he learned to drive before he moved here?
   (¿Él había aprendido a conducir antes de mudarse aquí?)

5. Had we met each other before the party?
   (¿Nosotros ya nos habíamos conocido antes de la fiesta?)

LESSON 6.3: The Future Perfect Tense

The Future Perfect tense is used to describe **an action that will have been completed before a specific time** or event in the future.

✏️ **Learner Tip:** The Future Perfect tense is formed by **will have + past participle** of the verb

Example:

By next week, **she will have finished** the project.

(The finishing of the project will be completed before next week.)

Common Verbs Conjugations in Future Perfect Tense

English Verb	Future Perfect Example	Spanish Translation
do	We **will have** done	Habremos hecho
finish	I **will have** finish**ed**	Habré terminado
go	She **will have** gone	Ella habrá ido
have	They **will have had**	Ellos habrán tenido
make	They **will have** ma**de**	Ellas habrán hecho
see	You **will have** seen	Habrás visto
take	I **will have** tak**en**	Habré tomado
write	He **will have** writ**ten**	Él habrá escrito

Activity 6.7: Fill in the Blank with Future Perfect Verbs

Directions: Complete the sentences using the Future Perfect form of the verb in parentheses.

Example:

> **Question:** By 5 p.m. tomorrow, they _____ (complete) the exam.
>
> **Answer:** By 5 p.m. tomorrow, **they will have completed** the exam.

1. By next month, I _____ (finish) my book.
   (El mes que viene habré terminado mi libro.)

2. She _____ (write) five reports by Friday.
   (Ella habrá escrito cinco informes para el viernes.)

3. We _____ (go) to Paris twice by the end of the year.
   (Nosotros habremos ido a París dos veces para finales de año).

4. He _____ (see) that movie before it leaves theaters.
   (Él habrá visto esa película antes de que salga de los cines.)

5. You _____ (do) all your chores by dinner time.
   (Tú habrás hecho todos tus quehaceres para la hora de la cena.)

6. They _____ (have) the house painted by next week.
   (Ellos habrán pintado la casa para la próxima semana.)

7. I _____ (make) all the arrangements by tomorrow.
   (Yo habré hecho todos los arreglos para mañana.)

8. By then, she _____ (take) the test three times.
   (Para entonces, ella habrá tomado el examen tres veces.)

Activity 6.8: Oral Answers Using the Future Perfect Tense

Directions: Answer aloud each question with the correct form of the Future Perfect tense.

Example:

> **Question:** Will you have eaten dinner by the time I arrive to pick you up?

> **Answer:** No (or Yes), I will not have eaten dinner by the time you arrive.

1. Will you have finished your work by 6 p.m.?
(¿Habrás terminado tu trabajo para las 6 p.m.?)

2. Will she have arrived before the meeting starts?
(¿Habrá llegado ella antes de que empiece la reunión?)

3. Will they have completed the project by next week?
(¿Habrán completado el proyecto para la próxima semana?)

4. Will we have learned everything by the end of the course?
(¿Habremos aprendido todo para el final del curso?)

5. Will he have called you by tomorrow?
(¿Te habrá llamado él para mañana?)

Activity 6.9: Oral Answers Using the Future Perfect Tense with Different Subjects

Directions: Answer aloud each question with the correct form of the Future Perfect Tense Verb.

Example:

> Question: **Will you have finished** by Thursday?

> Answer: Yes, I will have finished it by Thursday evening.

1. Will I have finished my homework by tonight?
   (¿Habré terminado mi tarea para esta noche?)

2. Will you have visited the new museum by next week?
   (¿Habrás visitado el nuevo museo para la próxima semana?)

3. Will he have arrived before the meeting starts?
   (¿Habrá llegado él antes de que empiece la reunión?)

4. Will she have completed the report by tomorrow?
   (¿Habrá ella terminado el informe para mañana?)

5. Will they have moved to their new house by the end of the month?
   (¿Habrán ellos mudado a su nueva casa para fin de mes?)

CHAPTER 7

Intermediate English Grammar: The Perfect Progressive Tenses

Perfect Progressive tenses in English, also known as Perfect Continuous tenses, describe actions that started in the past and continued to the present, into the future, or are ongoing.

- **Present Perfect Progressive:** actions **started in the past and are continuing or** recent actions that **have relevance to the present**.

- **Past Perfect Progressive:** actions that were ongoing or in progress at a specific time in the past.

- **Future Perfect Progressive:** actions that will have been ongoing for a duration of time before a specific point in the future.

LESSON 7.1: The Present Perfect Progressive Tense

The Present Perfect Progressive tense (also known as the Present Perfect Continuous tense) is used to describe an action that **started in the past and is still continuing** or an action that **was happening recently and has relevance to the present**.

🖊 **Learner Tip:** The structure of the Present Perfect Progressive tense is formed like this: **have/has + been + present participle (-ing form)**

(I/you/we/they → have been, he/she/it → has been)

Common Present Perfect Progressive Tense Verbs

English Verb	Present Perfect Progressive	Spanish
do	have/has been doing	he/ha estado haciendo
go	have/has been going	he/ha estado yendo
have	have/has been having	he/ha estado teniendo
make	have/has been making	he/ha estado haciendo / creando

Activity 7.1: Fill in the Blank with the Present Perfect Progressive Tense

Directions: Complete the sentences with the correct Present Perfect Progressive form of the verb in parentheses.

Examples:

I have been studying all day.

She has been working at the hospital since 2019.

1. I _____ _____ (have) a hard time sleeping lately.
   (He___ ___ problemas para dormir últimamente.)

2. She _____ _____ (do) a lot of exercise this month.
   (Ella ___ ___ ___ mucho ejercicio este mes.)

3. They _____ _____ (go) to that café every morning.
   (Ellos ___ ___ ___ a ese café cada mañana.)

4. We _____ _____ (make) plans for the weekend.
   (Hemos ___ ___ planes para el fin de semana.)

Activity7.2: Oral Questions with the Present Perfect Progressive Tense

Directions: Answer aloud the following questions with the Present Perfect Progressive tense.

Example:

>   **Question:** How long **have you been learning** Spanish?

>   **Answer: I have been learning** Spanish for three years.

1. How long have you been studying English?
   (¿Cuánto tiempo has estado estudiando inglés?)

2. What have you been doing today?
   (¿Qué has estado haciendo hoy?)

3. Have you been feeling okay lately?
   (¿Has estado sintiéndote bien últimamente?)

4. Have you been working on any new projects?
   (¿Has estado trabajando en algún proyecto nuevo?)

Activity 7.3: Present Perfect Progressive Tense Oral Answers with Different Subjects

Directions: Respond aloud to each question with the proper form of the Present Perfect Progressive verb.

Example:

>   **Question:** What have they been doing since morning?

>   **Answer:** They have been working on the new project since morning.

1. Have I been talking too much
    (¿He estado hablando demasiado?)

2. Have you been exercising regularly?
    (¿Has estado haciendo ejercicio regularmente?)

3. Has he been working late this week?
    (¿Él ha estado trabajando hasta tarde esta semana?)

4. Has she been learning a new language?
    (¿Ella ha estado aprendiendo un nuevo idioma?)

5. Has it been raining all day?
    (¿Ha estado lloviendo todo el día?)

6. Have we been doing this correctly?
    (¿Hemos estado haciendo esto correctamente?)

7. Have they been waiting for a long time?
    (¿Han estado esperando mucho tiempo?)

LESSON 7.2: The Past Perfect Progress Tense

The Past Perfect Progressive tense (also called the Past Perfect Continuous tense) describes an **ongoing action in the past that has ended or has been interrupted by another action or point in the past** Although this tense can be useful in some situations, it is not used as often as other tenses.

In English, the structure is formed by: **had been+ present participle (verb + -ing).** In Spanish, however, it is formed by combining the imperfect tense of **haber + the past participle estado + the gerund (-ando/-iendo)** of the main verb.

Examples:

She **had been studying** when the phone rang.

They **had been watching** TV <u>when</u> the phone rang.

(The actions were in progress when another action happened.)

🖊 **Learner Tip:** The "had been" part of the construction does not change with the subject/pronoun.

Common Verbs with Past Perfect Progressive Conjugations

English Verb	Past Perfect Progressive (I/You/HeWe/They)	Spanish Translation (Past Perfect Progressive)
come	had been coming	Yo había estado viniendo
		Tú habías estado viniendo
		Nosotros habíamos estado viniendo
		Él/Ella había estado viniendo
		Ellos habían estado viniendo
do make	had been doing had been making	Yo había estado haciendo
		Tú habías estado haciendo
		Nosotros habíamos estado haciendo
		Él/Ella había estado haciendo
		Ellos habían estado haciendo
eat	had been eating	Yo había estado comiendo
		Tú habías estado comiendo
		Nosotros habíamos estado comiendo
		Él/Ella había estado comiendo

English Verb	Past Perfect Progressive (I/You/HeWe/They)	Spanish Translation (Past Perfect Progressive)
		Ellos habían estado comiendo
go	had been going	Yo había estado yendo
		Tú habías estado yendo
		Nosotros habíamos estado yendo
		Él/Ella había estado yendo
		Ellos habían estado yendo
have	had been having	Yo había estado teniendo
		Tú habías estado teniendo
		Nosotros habíamos estado teniendo
		Él/Ella había estado teniendo
		Ellos habían estado teniendo
read	had been reading	Yo había estado leyendo
		Tú habías estado leyendo
		Nosotros habíamos estado leyendo
		Él/Ella había estado leyendo
		Ellos habían estado leyendo
write	had been writing	Yo había estado escribiendo
		Tú habías estado escribiendo
		Nosotros habíamos estado escribiendo
		Él/Ella habías estado escribiendo
		Ellos habían estado escribiendo

Activity 7.4: Fill in the Blank with the Past Perfect Progressive Tense.

Directions: Complete the sentences with the correct Past Perfect Progressive form of the verb in parentheses.

Example:

She _____ (read) a book when I called her.

She **had been reading** a book <u>when</u> I called her.

1. I _____ (eat) dinner when the doorbell rang.
   (Yo ____ ____ cenando cuando sonó el timbre.)

2. They _____ (go) to the park while it was raining.
   (Ellos____ ____ ____ al parque mientras llovía.)

3. We _____ (do) our homework at 7 p.m. yesterday.
   (Nosotros ____ ____ ____nuestra tarea a las 7 p.m. ayer.)

4. He _____ (have) a meeting when I arrived.
   (Él ____ ____ ____ una reunión cuando llegué.)

5. You _____ (make) a lot of noise last night.
   (Tú ____ ____ ____ mucho ruido anoche mientras yo dormía.)

6. She _____ (come) to the library every day while I worked out at the gym.
   (Ella ____ ____ ____ a la biblioteca todos los días mientras yo hacía ejercicio en el gimnasio.)

7. The children _____ (write) stories in class.
   (Los niños ____ ____ ____ historias en clase mientras el maestro preparaba la siguiente.)

8. My parents _____ (read) the newspaper in the morning.
   (Mis padres ____ ____ ____ el periódico por la mañana mientras yo hacía el desayuno.)

LESSON 7.3: The Future Perfect Progressive Tense

The Future Perfect Progressive tense describes an **action that will have been ongoing for a duration of time before a specific point in the future**. It emphasizes the continuity of an action up until that future moment.

✏️ **Learner Tip:** The Future Perfect Progressive tense is formed by **will have been + present participle (verb + -ing)**

Example:

> By next year, **I will have been working** at this company for five years. (The action "working" will have been continuing for five years up to that point.)

Common Verb Conjugations in Future Perfect Progressive Tense

English Verb	Future Perfect Progressive Example	Spanish Translation
live	He **will have been** living	El habrá estado viviendo
read	I **will have been** reading	Habré estado leyendo
run	You **will have been** running	Habrás estado corriendo
study	She **will have been** studying	Ella habrá estado estudiando
teach	I **will have been** teaching	Habré estado enseñando
travel	They **will have been** traveling	Ellos habrán estado viajando
work	I **will have been** working	Habré estado trabajando
write	We **will have been** writing	Habremos estado escribiendo

Activity 7.5: Fill in the Blank with Future Perfect Progressive Verbs

Directions: Complete the sentences using the Future Perfect Progressive form of the verb in parentheses.

Example:

> **Question:** By next month, she _____ (teach) at the school for ten years.
>
> **Answer:** By next month, **she will have been teaching** at the school for ten years.

1. By December, I _____ (work) here for three years.
   (Para diciembre, ___ ___ ___ aquí por tres años.)

2. Next week, they _____ (travel) for 24 hours straight.
   (La próxima semana, ellos ___ ___ ___ durante 24 horas seguidas.)

3. By 2026, we _____ (live) in this city for a decade.
   (Para 2026, ___ ___ ___ en esta ciudad por una década.)

4. At 7 p.m. tonight, he _____ (run) for an hour.
   (A las 7 p.m. de esta noche, él ___ ___ ___ por una hora.)

5. She _____ (study) all day by the time the exam starts.
   (Ella ___ ___ ___ todo el día cuando empiece el examen.)

6. By this time tomorrow, you _____ (write) for five hours.
   (Para esta hora mañana, ___ ___ ___ por cinco horas.)

7. They _____ (read) the book for two weeks by Friday.
   (Para el viernes, ellos ___ ___ ___ el libro por dos semanas.)

8. By next summer, I _____ (teach) at the university for 15 years.
   (Para el próximo verano, h ___ ___ ___ en la universidad por 15 años.)

Activity 7.6: Oral Answers Using the Future Perfect Progressive Tense

Directions: Answer aloud each question with the correct form of the Future Perfect Progressive tense.

Example:

> **Question:** By next December, how long will you have been celebrating Christmas in Phoenix?

> **Answer:** By next December, **I will have been celebrating** Christmas in Phoenix for 20 years.

1. How long will you have been working at your job by next year?
   (¿Cuánto tiempo habrás estado trabajando en tu trabajo para el próximo año?)

2. Will she have been studying English for five years by then?
   (¿Ella habrá estado estudiando inglés por cinco años para entonces?)

3. Will they have been living in this city for a decade soon?
   (¿Ellos habrán estado viviendo en esta ciudad por una década pronto?)

4. Will we have been waiting for more than an hour by the time the bus arrives?
   (¿Habremos estado esperando por más de una hora cuando llegué el autobús?)

5. Will he have been practicing the piano all afternoon?
   (¿Él habrá estado practicando el piano toda la tarde?)

Activity 7.7: Oral Answers Using the Future Perfect Progressive Tense with Different Subjects

Directions: Answer aloud each question with the correct form of the Future Perfect Progressive tense verb.

Example:

> **Question:** By next June, how long will you have been working at your current job?
>
> **Answer:** By next June, **I will have been working** at my current job for five years.

1. Will I have been working here for five years by next month?
   (¿Habré estado trabajando aquí por cinco años para el próximo mes?)

2. Will you have been studying all night before the exam?
   (¿Habrás estado estudiando toda la noche antes del examen?)

3. Will he have been traveling for a long time by the end of the trip?
   (¿Él habrá estado viajando por mucho tiempo para el final del viaje?)

4. Will she have been living in that city for ten years soon?
   (¿Ella habrá estado viviendo en esa ciudad por diez años pronto?)

5. Will they have been waiting for us when we arrive?
   (¿Habrán estado esperándonos cuando lleguemos?)

CHAPTER 8

Advanced English Grammar: Conditional Verb Tenses

LESSON 8.1: The Simple Conditional Tense

The Simple Conditional tense is used to describe actions that **would happen under certain conditions** or in hypothetical situations. It often expresses desires, possibilities, or polite requests. It is formed by **would + base form of the verb.**

Example:

> **I would go** to the party <u>if</u> I had time. (Iría a la fiesta si tuviera tiempo.)
>
> (The action "go" depends on the condition "if I had time.")

🖉 **Learner Tip:** In English, **would + base verb** does not change with the subject/pronoun.

Common Verb Conjugations with Simple Conditional Tense

English Verb	English Simple Conditional	Spanish Simple Conditional
come	**I would** come	Yo vendría
do	**We would** do	Haríamos
eat	**She would** eat	Ella comería
go	**I would** go	Yo iría

English Verb	English Simple Conditional	Spanish Simple Conditional
have	**You would** have	Tendrías
make	**They would make**	Ellos harían
see	**He would** see	Él vería
take	**I would** take	Yo tomaría

Activity 8.1: Fill in the Blank Using the Simple Conditional Tense

Directions: Complete the sentences using the Simple Conditional form of the verb in parentheses.

Example:

> **Question:** He _____ (go) to the beach if it were warm.
>
> **Answer:** **He would go** to the beach if it were warm.

1. I _____ (go) to the beach if it's sunny.
   (Yo ____ ____ a la playa si hubiera hecho sol.)

2. They _____ (eat) dinner earlier if they were hungry.
   (Ellos ____ ____ antes si hubieran tenido hambre.)

3. We _____ (see) the movie if we had tickets.
   (Nosotros ____ ____ la película si hubiéramos tenido entradas.)

4. He _____ (have) more time if he didn't work late.
   (Él ____ ____ más tiempo si no hubiera trabajado hasta tarde.)

5. You _____ (do) well if you studied harder.
   (Te ____ ____ bien si hubieras estudiado.)

6. She _____ (make) a cake if it was her birthday.
   (Ella ____ ____ un pastel si fuera su cumpleaños.)

7. We _____ (come) to the party if we are invited.
   (Nosotros ___ ___ a la fiesta si nos hubieran invitado.)

8. I _____ (take) a taxi if I missed the bus.
   (Yo ___ ___ un taxi si hubiera perdido el autobús.)

Activity 8.2: Oral Answers Using the Simple Conditional Tense

Directions: Answer these questions aloud using the correct Simple Conditional tense of the verb.

Example:

> **Question:** What would you do if you won the lottery?
>
> **Answer:** I **would buy** a house and travel the world <u>if I won</u> the lottery.

1. If you could live anywhere, where would you live?
   (Si pudieras vivir en cualquier lugar, ¿dónde vivirías?)

2. Would you help me if I asked you?
   (¿Me ayudarías si te lo pidiera?)

3. What would you eat if you were hungry right now?
   (¿Qué comerías si tuvieras hambre ahora mismo?)

4. If you met a celebrity, what would you say?
   (Si conocieras a una celebridad, ¿qué dirías?)

5. Would you work abroad if you had the chance?
   (¿Trabajarías en el extranjero si tuvieras la oportunidad?)

LESSON 8.2: The Conditional Progressive Tense

The Conditional Progressive tense describes **an action that would be in progress under certain hypothetical conditions**. It emphasizes that the action would be ongoing at a specific moment in the imagined situation. It is formed by: **would be + present participle (verb + -ing).**

Example:

> If I <u>were</u> home, **I would be watching** TV right now.
> (The action "watching" would be happening if the condition were true.)

🖉 **Learner Tip:** In English, **would be + (verb + -ing).** does not change with the subject.

Common Verb Conjugations with Conditional Progressive Tense

English Verb	Conditional Progressive	Spanish Translation
eat	She would be eating	Ella estaría comiendo
go	He would be going	Él estaría yendo
play	They would be playing	Ellos estarían jugando
read	We would be reading	Estaríamos leyendo
study	You would be studying	Estarías estudiando
travel	I would be traveling	Yo estaría viajando
work	I would be working	Yo estaría trabajando
write	They would be writing	Ellos estarían escribiendo

Activity 8.3: Fill in the Blank Using the Conditional Progressive Tense

Directions: Complete the sentences using the Conditional Progressive form of the verb in parentheses.

Example:

> **Question:** If she had more time, she _____ (read) that book right now.

> **Answer:** If she had more time, she **would be reading** that book right now.

1. If I were there, I _____ (work) with you.
(Si yo estuviera allí, estaría trabajando contigo.)

2. They _____ (eat) dinner if they weren't so busy.
(Cenarían si no estuvieran tan ocupados.)

3. You _____ (study) more if you had fewer distractions.
(Estudiarías más si tuvieras menos distracciones.)

4. He _____ (go) to the gym if he felt better.
(Iría al gimnasio si se sintiera mejor.)

5. We _____ (play) outside if it weren't raining.
(Nosotros jugaríamos afuera si no estuviera lloviendo.)

6. She _____ (write) a letter if she had time.
(Escribiría una carta si tuviera tiempo.)

7. I _____ (travel) more if I had enough money.
(Viajaría más si tuviera suficiente dinero.)

8. They _____ (read) the report if it were important.
(Habrían leído el informe si fuera importante.)

Activity 8.4: Oral Answers with the Conditional Progressive Tense

Directions: Answer these questions aloud with the proper Conditional

Progressive verb.

Example:

> **Question:** What **would you be doing** <u>if you weren't</u> at work right
> now?
>
> **Answer:** I **would be relaxing** at the beach.

1. What would you be doing right now if you weren't talking to me?
   (¿Qué estarías haciendo ahora mismo si no estuvieras hablando
   conmigo?)

2. Would you be working if you had the chance to take a vacation?
   (¿Estarías trabajando si tuvieras la oportunidad de tomar vacaciones?)

3. If you were living in another country, would you be studying a new
   language?
   (Si vivieras en otro país, ¿estarías estudiando un nuevo idioma?)

4. Would she be waiting for us if we were late?
   (¿Ella estaría esperándonos si llegáramos tarde?)

5. Would they be traveling this summer if there were no restrictions?
   (¿Estarían ellos viajando este verano si no hubiera restricciones?)

LESSON 8.3: The Conditional Perfect Tense

The Conditional Perfect tense expresses an **action that would have happened in the past** <u>under certain hypothetical conditions</u>. It is used to talk about unreal or imagined past situations. It is formed by: **would have + past participle.**

Example:

If I <u>had studied</u> more, I _____ (pass) the exam.

If I <u>had studied</u> more, I **would have** passed the exam.

(The action "pass" did not happen, but it would have if the condition had been met.)

✏️ **Learner Tip:** In English, **would have + past participle** does not change with the subject.

Common Verb Conjugations with Conditional Perfect Tense

English Verb	Conditional Perfect	Spanish Translation
come	I would have come	Yo habría venido
do	We would have done	Habríamos hecho
eat	She would have eaten	Ella habría comido
go	I would have gone	Yo habría ido
have	You would have had	Habrías tenido
make	They would have made	Ellos habrían hecho
see	He would have seen	Él habría visto
take	I would have taken	Yo habría tomado

Activity 8.5: Fill in the Blank Using the Conditional Perfect Tense

Directions: Complete the sentences using the Conditional Perfect form of the verb in parentheses.

Example:

    Question: If she had left earlier, she _____ (arrive) on time.

    Answer: If she had left earlier, she **would have arrived** on time.

1. If I had seen him, I _____ (talk) to him.
   (Si lo hubiera visto, habría hablado con él)

2. They _____ (eat) the food if they had been hungry.
   (Habrían comido la comida si hubieran tenido hambre.)

3. We _____ (go) to the concert if we had bought tickets.
   (Habríamos ido al concierto si hubiéramos comprado las entradas.)

4. He _____ (have) more money if he had worked harder.
   (Habría tenido más dinero si hubiera trabajado más duro.)

5. You _____ (do) better if you had practiced more.
   (Lo habrías hecho mejor si hubieras practicado más.)

6. She _____ (make) the decision if she had known the facts.
   (Ella habría tomado la decisión, si hubiera sabido los hechos.)

7. I _____ (come) earlier if I had finished my work.
   (Habría venido antes si hubiera terminado mi trabajo.)

8. They _____ (take) the bus if it hadn't rained.
   (Habrían tomado el autobús si no hubiera llovido.)

Activity 8.6: Oral Answers Using the Conditional Perfect Tense

Directions: Answer the questions aloud using the Conditional Perfect tense.

Example:

> **Question:** If you had stayed in the program, how long would you have been studying medicine?
>
> **Answer:** I **would have completed** my degree by now.

1. Would you have traveled more if you had more money?
   (¿Habrías viajado más si tuvieras más dinero?)

2. Would she have accepted the job if it had been offered to her?
   (¿Habría aceptado ella el trabajo si se lo hubieran ofrecido?)

3. Would they have moved to a new city if they had found better jobs?
   (¿Se habrían mudado a una nueva ciudad si hubieran encontrado mejores trabajos?)

4. Would you have studied another language if you had had more time?
   (¿Habrías estudiado otro idioma si hubieras tenido más tiempo?)

5. Would he have called you if he had remembered your birthday?
   (¿Te habría llamado él si hubiera recordado tu cumpleaños?)

LESSON 8.4: The Conditional Perfect Progressive Tense

The Conditional Perfect Progressive tense describes an **action that would have been ongoing for a duration of time under certain hypothetical past conditions.** It emphasizes the continuous action that really didn't happen. It is formed by **would have been + present participle (verb + -ing)**.

Example:

If she <u>had arrived earlier</u>, she **would have been working** for two hours by then.

(The action "working" would have been in progress for a certain time under the condition.)

✏️ **Learner Tip: In English, would have been + (verb + -ing)** does not change with the subject.

Common Verb Conjugations with Conditional Perfect Progressive

English Verb	Conditional Perfect Progressive	Spanish Translation
live	He would have been living	Él habría estado viviendo
read	I would have been reading	Yo habría estado leyendo
run	You would have been running	Habrías estado corriendo
study	She would have been studying	Ella habría estado estudiando
teach	They would have been teaching	Ellos habrías estado enseñando
travel	They would have been traveling	Ellos habrían estado viajando
work	I would have been working	Yo habría estado trabajando
write	We would have been writing	Habríamas estado escribiendo

Activity 8.7: Fill in the Blank Using the Conditional Perfect Progressive Tense

Directions: Complete the sentences using the Conditional Perfect

Progressive form of the verb in parentheses.

Example:

Question: If I hadn't been sick, I _____ (study) for hours.

Answer: If I hadn't been sick, I **would have been studying** for hours.

1. If they had arrived earlier, they _____ (work) all day.
(Si hubieran llegado antes,—- —- todo el día.)

2. She _____ (travel) for months if she hadn't changed her plans.
(Ella ___ ___ durante meses si no hubiera cambiado sus planes.)

3. I _____ (run) every morning if I hadn't been injured.
(Yo ___ ___ todas las mañanas si no me hubiera lesionado.)

4. By then, we _____ (live) here for five years if we hadn't moved.
(Para entonces, ___ ___ aquí durante cinco años si no nos hubiéramos mudado.)

5. He _____ (write) his novel if he hadn't gotten distracted.
(Él___ ___ su novela si no se hubiera distraído.)

6. You _____ (study) more if you hadn't missed the class.
(Tu___ ___ más si no te hubieras saltado la clase.)

7. They _____ (teach) at the school longer if they hadn't retired.
(Ellos ___ ___ en la escuela durante más tiempo si no se hubieran jubilado.)

8. She _____ (read) the entire series if she hadn't been so busy.
(Ella ___ ___ la serie completa si no hubiera estado tan ocupada.)

Activity 8.8: Oral Answers Using the Conditional Perfect Progressive Tense

Directions: Answer aloud each question using the Conditional Perfect

Progressive tense.

Example:

> **Question:** <u>If she hadn't moved</u> to another city, how long would she have been working at the company?
>
> **Answer:** She **would have been working** at the company for ten years if she hadn't moved.

1. Would you have been working here if you hadn't moved?
   (¿Habrías estado trabajando aquí si no te hubieras mudado?)

2. What would you have been doing if you hadn't gone to college?
   (¿Qué habrías estado haciendo si no hubieras ido a la universidad?)

3. Would she have been studying medicine if her grades had been better?
   (¿Ella habría estado estudiando medicina si sus notas hubieran sido mejores?)

4. Would we have been living abroad if we had taken that job offer?
   (¿Habríamos estado viviendo en el extranjero si hubiéramos aceptado esa oferta de trabajo?)

5. Would he have been practicing more if he had had the time?
   (¿Él habría estado practicando más si hubiera tenido tiempo?)

6. Would you have been feeling better if you had rested more?
   (¿Te habrías estado sintiendo mejor si hubieras descansado más?)

7. Would they have been saving money if they hadn't gone on vacation?
   (¿Habrían estado ahorrando dinero si no se hubieran ido de vacaciones?)

CHAPTER 9
Vocabulary

LESSON 9.1: Classroom Objects

The following is a list of 30 classroom objects in English with their Spanish translations, including the article "the":

1. The backpack (La mochila)
2. The binder (El archivador)
3. The board (La pizarra)
4. The book (El libro)
5. The calculator (La calculadora)
6. The calendar (El calendario)
7. The chair (La silla)
8. The clock (El reloj)
9. The computer (La computadora)
10. The crayon (El crayón)
11. The desk (El escritorio)
12. The dictionary (El diccionario)
13. The eraser (El borrador)
14. The folder (La carpeta)
15. The glue (El pegamento)
16. The highlighter (El resaltador)
17. The Internet (La Internet)
18. The map (El mapa)
19. The marker (El marcador)
20. The notebook (El cuaderno)
21. The paper (El papel)
22. The pen (El bolígrafo)
23. The pencil (El lápiz)
24. The projector (El proyector)
25. The ruler (La regla)
26. The scissors (Las tijeras)
27. The sharpener (El sacapuntas)
28. The stapler (La grapadora)
29. The table (La mesa)
30. The tape (La cinta adhesiva)

LESSON 9.2: Rooms in the House

Below is a list of 30 common rooms and areas in a house, with the article "the" in English and Spanish:

1. The living room (La sala)
2. The kitchen (La cocina)
3. The bedroom (El dormitorio)
4. The bathroom (El baño)
5. The dining room (El comedor)
6. The hallway (El pasillo)
7. The garage (El garaje)
8. The basement (El sótano)
9. The attic (El ático)
10. The laundry room (El cuarto de lavado)
11. The office (La oficina)
12. The guest room (El cuarto de huéspedes)
13. The closet (El armario)
14. The pantry (La despensa)
15. The balcony (El balcón)
16. The patio (El patio)
17. The yard (El patio / El jardín)
18. The garden (El jardín)
19. The stairs (Las escaleras)
20. The entryway (La entrada)
21. The foyer (El vestíbulo)
22. The porch (El porche)
23. The terrace (La terraza)
24. The playroom (El cuarto de juegos)
25. The study (El estudio)
26. The den (La sala de estar)
27. The mudroom (El recibidor)
28. The sunroom (El cuarto soleado)
29. The storage room (El cuarto de almacenamiento)
30. The roof (El techo)

LESSON 9.3: Household Appliances

The following is a list of 30 classroom objects in English with their Spanish translations, including the article "the":

1. The refrigerator
    (El refrigerador)

2. The stove
    (La estufa)

3. The oven
    (El horno)

4. The microwave
    (El microondas)

5. The dishwasher
    (El lavavajillas)

6. The washing machine
    (La lavadora)

7. The dryer
    (La secadora)

8. The vacuum cleaner
    (La aspiradora)

9. The fan
    (El ventilador)

10. The air conditioner
    (El aire acondicionado)

11. The heater
    (El calentador)

12. The television
    (El televisor)

13. The radio
    (La radio)

14. The computer
    (La computadora)

15. The printer
    (La impresora)

16. The blender
    (La licuadora)

17. The toaster
    (La tostadora)

18. The coffee maker
    (La cafetera)

19. The electric kettle
    (La tetera eléctrica)

20. The iron
    (La plancha)

21. The hair dryer
    (El secador de pelo)

22. The lamp
    (La lámpara)

23. The ceiling fan
    (El ventilador de techo)

24. The water heater
    (El calentador de agua)

25. The freezer
    (El congelador)

26. The garbage disposal
    (El triturador de basura)

27. The humidifier
    (El humidificador)

28. The dehumidifier
    (El deshumidificador)

29. The smoke detector
    (El detector de humo)

30. The doorbell
    (El timbre)

LESSON 9.4: The Family

Here are 30 common names for family members, including the article "the":

1. The mother (La madre)
2. The father (El padre)
3. The parents (Los padres)
4. The mom (La mamá)
5. The dad (El papá)
6. The son (El hijo)
7. The daughter (La hija)
8. The child (El niño / La niña)
9. The children (Los niños)
10. The brother (El hermano)
11. The sister (La hermana)
12. The siblings (Los hermanos)
13. The grandfather (El abuelo)
14. The grandmother (La abuela)
15. The grandparents (Los abuelos)
16. The uncle (El tío)
17. The aunt (La tía)
18. The cousin (El primo / La prima)
19. The nephew (El sobrino)
20. The niece (La sobrina)
21. The husband (El esposo)
22. The wife (La esposa)
23. The partner (La pareja)
24. The stepfather (El padrastro)
25. The stepmother (La madrastra)
26. The stepson (El hijastro)
27. The stepdaughter (La hijastra)
28. The brother-in-law (El cuñado)
29. The sister-in-law (La cuñada)
30. The family (La familia)

CHAPTER 10

Essential Conversations

LESSON 10.1: Beginner & Intermediate Level Conversation (Present Tense): At the Grocery Store

Clerk: Hello! Can I help you find something?

Customer: Yes, please. Where do you keep the eggs?

Clerk: They are in the refrigerated section, next to the milk.

Customer: Thanks! And do you sell fresh bread?

Clerk: Yes, we do. The bakery is at the back of the store.

Customer: Great. I also need some apples. Are they fresh today?

Clerk: Yes, they are very fresh. We get new produce every morning.

Customer: Perfect. I'll take six. Do you have paper bags?

Clerk: Yes, they're at the checkout counter.

Customer: Thank you. I think I'm ready to pay.

Clerk: No problem. You can go to register three.

Customer: Thanks for your help!

Clerk: You're welcome! Have a nice day.

LESSON 10.2: Beginner & Intermediate Level Conversation (Present Tense): At the Post Office

Clerk: Good morning! How can I help you today?

Customer: Hi. I want to send this package to New York.

Clerk: Okay. Do you want standard or express shipping?

Customer: What's the difference?

Clerk: Standard delivery takes five to seven days. Express delivery arrives in two days.

Customer: I'll choose express, please.

Clerk: Great. Can you place the package on the scale?

Customer: Sure. Here it is.

Clerk: It weighs 2.3 kilograms. That will be $18.75.

Customer: Do you accept credit cards?

Clerk: Yes, we do.

Customer: Perfect. I'm paying with my card.

Clerk: Done! Here's your receipt and tracking number.

Customer: Thanks! Have a nice day.

Clerk: You, too!

LESSON 10.3: Intermediate & Advanced Level Conversation (Future Tense): At a Concert

7Emma: Are you excited about the concert tonight?

Liam: Yes! It's going to be amazing. What time will it start?

Emma: The band will come on stage at 8 p.m.

Liam: Great. Will we have good seats?

Emma: Yes, we bought them early, so we'll be close to the stage.

Liam: Awesome. Will they play your favorite song?

Emma: I hope so! I'm sure they'll perform all their hits.

Liam: Will we meet the others there?

Emma: Yes, they'll arrive a bit earlier to save our spots.

Liam: Perfect. This will be a night to remember!

LESSON 10.4: Advanced Level Conversation (Multiple Tenses): At the Airport

Passenger: Good morning. I missed my flight. Can you help me?

Agent: Good morning. Yes, I can. Where were you flying to?

Passenger: I was flying to Chicago.

Agent: May I see your ticket and passport, please?

Passenger: Yes, here they are.

Agent: Thank you. Did you pack your bags yourself?

Passenger: Yes, I did.

Agent: Did you check in online?

Passenger: No, I didn't. I wasn't sure how to do it.

Agent: That's okay. I checked you in just now. Did you bring any carry-or luggage?

Passenger: Yes, I brought a small backpack.

Agent: Great. Your old flight boarded Gate 12, and it departed on time. I've booked you on a new flight going to Chicago. It boards from Gate 13 and will leave at 11:30 a.m.

Passenger: Thank you so much!

Agent: You're welcome. Have a safe trip!

ENGLISH VERB TENSES

English Verb Tenses: Overview

Tense Type	Usage	English	Spanish
Present Simple	Habit, fact, general truth	I eat	Yo como
Present Progressive	Action happening now or around now	I am eating	Estoy comiendo
Present Perfect	Action completed at an unspecified time	I have eaten	He comido
Present Perfect Progressive	Action started in the past, still continuing	I have been eating breakfast.	He estado comiendo
Past Simple	Completed action in the past	I ate	Comí
Past Progressive	Ongoing action at a specific past time	I was eating	Estaba comiendo
Past Perfect	Action completed before another past action	I had eaten	Había comido
Past Perfect Progressive	Duration of an action before another past event	I had been eating	Había estado comiendo
Future Simple	Action that will happen in the future	I will eat	Comeré
Future Progressive	Ongoing action at a future time	I will be eating	Estaré comiendo
Future Perfect	Action completed before a future time	I will have eaten	Habré comido

Tense Type	Usage	English	Spanish
Future Perfect Progressive	Duration before a future event	I will have been eating	Habré estado comiendo
Conditional Simple	Action that would happen under certain conditions	I would eat	Comeríamos
Conditional Progressive	Action that would be in progress under certain conditions	I would be eating	Estaría comiendo
Conditional Perfect	Action that would have happened in the past under certain conditions	I would have eaten	Habría comido
Conditional Perfect Progressive	Action that would have been ongoing under certain past conditions.	I would have been eating	Habría estado comiendo

English Present Tenses

English Tense	Spanish Tense	English Example (to eat)	Spanish Translation
Present Simple	Presente	I eat lunch every day.	Yo como almuerzo todos los días.
Present Progressive	Presente Continuo	I am eating lunch right now.	Estoy comiendo almuerzo ahora.
Present Perfect	Pretérito Perfecto	I have eaten lunch.	He comido almuerzo.
Present Perfect Progressive	Pretérito Perfecto Continuo	I have been eating lunch for an hour.	He estado comiendo almuerzo por una hora.

English Past Tenses

English Tense	Spanish Tense	English Example (to eat)	Spanish Translation
Past Simple	Pretérito Indefinido	I ate lunch yesterday.	Comí almuerzo ayer.
Past Progressive	Pretérito Imperfecto Continuo	I was eating lunch when you called.	Estaba comiendo almuerzo cuando me llamaste.
Past Perfect	Pretérito Pluscuamperfecto	I had eaten lunch before I left.	Había comido almuerzo antes de irme.
Past Perfect Progressive	Pretérito Pluscuamperfecto Continuo	I had been eating lunch for an hour when you called.	Había estado comiendo almuerzo por una hora cuando me llamaste.

English Future Tenses

English Tense	Spanish Tense	English Example (to eat)	Spanish Translation
Future Simple	Futuro Simple	I will eat lunch tomorrow.	Comeré almuerzo mañana.
Future Progressive	Futuro Continuo	I will be eating lunch at 12 p.m.	Estaré comiendo almuerzo a las 12 p.m.
Future Perfect	Futuro Perfecto	I will have eaten lunch by 1 p.m.	Habré comido almuerzo para la 1 p.m.
Future Perfect Progressive	Futuro Perfecto Continuo	I will have been eating lunch for an hour by 1 p.m.	Habré estado comiendo almuerzo por una hora para la 1 p.m.

English Conditional Tenses

English Tense	Spanish Tense	Example in English	Example in Spanish
Conditional Simple	Condicional Simple	I would eat lunch if I were hungry.	Comerí almuerzo si tuviera hambre.
Conditional Progressive	Condicional Continuo	I would be eating lunch if I were at home.	Estaría comiendo almuerzo si estuviera en casa.
Conditional Perfect	Condicional Perfecto	I would have eaten lunch if I had time.	Habría comido almuerzo si hubiera tenido tiempo.
Conditional Perfect Progressive	Condicional Perfecto Continuo	I would have been eating lunch if I had been at home.	Habría estado comiendo almuerzo si hubiera estado en casa.

PERSONAL DICTIONARY OF
NEW WORDS LEARNED

1. _____

2. _____

3. _____

4. _____

5. _____

6. _____

7. _____

8. _____

9. _____

10. _____

11. _____

12. _____

13. _____

14. _____

15. _____

16. _____

17. _____

18. _____

19. _____

20. _____

21. _____

22. _____

23. _____

24. _____

25. _____

26. _____

27. _____

28. _____

29. _____

30. _____

31. _____

32. _____

33. _____

34. _____

35. _____

36. _____

37. _____

38. _____

39. _____

40. _____

41. _____

42. _____

43. _____

44. _____

45. _____

46. _____

47. _____

48. _____

49. _____

50. _____

51. _____

52. _____

53. _____

54. _____

55. _____

56. _____

57. _____

58. _____

59. _____

60. _____

61. _____

62. _____

63. _____

64. _____

65. _____

66. _____

67. _____

68. _____

69. _____

70. _____

71. _____

72. _____

73. _____

74. _____

75. _____

76. _____

77. _____

78. _____

79. _____

80. _____

81. _____

82. _____

83. _____

84. _____

85. _____

86. _____

87. _____

88. _____

89. _____

90. _____

91. _____

92. _____

93. _____

94. _____

95. _____

96. _____

97. _____

98. _____

99. _____

100. _____

BIBLIOGRAPHY

Krashen, Stephen. D. Principles and Practice in Second Language Acquisition. Pergamon Press, 1982.

Krashen, Stephen. D. The Input Hypothesis: Issues and Implications. Longman, 1985.

Krashen, S. D., & Terrell, T. D. (1983). The natural approach: Language acquisition in the classroom. Pergamon.

Lichtman, K. (2014). Teaching Proficiency Through Reading and Storytelling (TPRS): An Input-Based Approach to Second Language Instruction. Xlibris Corporation.

Marzano, R. J., Pickering, D. J., & Pollock, J. E. (2001). Classroom instruction that works: Research-based strategies for increasing student achievement. Association for Supervision and Curriculum Development.

Ray, Blaine & Seely C. 2015. Fluency through TPR storytelling: Achieving real language acquisition in school (7th ed). Command Performance Language Institute.

ABOUT THE AUTHOR

Kecia Beasley Lindsey has educated students and business clients in bilingual skills for more than 25 years. She has taught bilingual education to children in elementary school through high school, as well as trained instructors.

After starting several language services companies, Beasley launched her company, EnglishAndSpanish2You.com, in 2020, providing in-person and online education to clients, with a goal of developing oral speaking skills in English and Spanish.

Whether training healthcare professionals or teaching school children, she has placed a high priority on creating a non-threatening and low-anxiety learning atmosphere, where students can focus on conversations in English and Spanish.

"I created 'English in a Bag' from my passion for teaching Spanish," Beasley said. "I want learners of all ages and skill levels to embrace the joy and empowerment of knowing a new language."